T0082777

SACRED, MUNDANE, PROFANE

SACRED, MUNDANE, PROFANE

A CONSTITUTIONAL PERSPECTIVE

Scott Rutledge

Algora Publishing
New York

Library of Congress Cataloging-in-Publication Data

Names: Rutledge, Walter Scott, author.
Title: Sacred, mundane, profane: a constitutional perspective / Walter
    Scott Rutledge.
Description: New York: Algora Publishing, [2021] | Includes
    bibliographical references. | Summary: "The Supreme Court's political
    power rivals that of Congress and the Presidency, and the Justices'
    ambitions often seem vast. The author argues that the Court has handed
    down decisions which are essentially religious in character, while
    speaking the language of constitutional interpretation, and in effect
    usurping the legislative power of Congress"— Provided by publisher.
Identifiers: LCCN 2020056581 (print) | LCCN 2020056582 (ebook) | ISBN
    9781628944495 (trade paperback) | ISBN 9781628944501 (hardcover) | ISBN
    9781628944518 (pdf)
Subjects: LCSH: United States. Supreme Court. | Judicial process—United
    States. | Political questions and judicial power—United States. |
    Religion and law—United States. | Constitutional law—Religious
    aspects.
Classification: LCC KF8748 . R887 2021 (print) | LCC KF8748 (ebook) | DDC
    347.73/26—dc23
LC record available at https://lccn.loc.gov/2020056581
LC ebook record available at https://lccn.loc.gov/2020056582

TABLE OF CONTENTS

INTRODUCTION

In 1976, the American Supreme Court pondered the future of capital punishment in the United States. Formally, the case before the Court concerned only one state government's pending execution of one man convicted of murder. The lawyers pleading for the condemned man, however, used the occasion to put the death penalty itself on trial. They urged the Court to declare judicially-ordered execution, under any circumstances whatever, constitutionally prohibited.

The appropriate punishment for a particular crime is a legal dispute; the fate of the practice of capital punishment involves much more than that. Should there be such a thing as death row at all? Or should executions, even for the most heinous crimes, be relegated to the proverbial dustbin of history? This is no mere quarrel among lawyers. Here lawyers can hardly help posing as social scientists or political philosophers. Here lawyers might easily find themselves arguing as if they were theologians.

Only two of the nine Justices on the Court in 1976 were ready to change their nation's law so boldly.[1] Did the Justices decide wisely? Poorly?

Here, however, let us shift the focus. Let us ask, rather: What kind of role or function would judges be taking on if they decided to abolish the death penalty? And conversely: When

---

[1] Gregg v. Georgia, 428 U.S. 153 (1976)

judges decline to do so in the face of principled opposition, in what character do they act?

Such questions may seem beside the point to those whose passions on the issue are intense. But a broader perspective might serve to educate, and perhaps to moderate, those very passions.

We can begin by reviewing the common patterns of disagreement between abolitionists and traditionalists. A representative of each can assist us with a concise rehearsal of various arguments often put forward.

Abolitionist: The trend is clear. As the number of executions steadily decreases, more and more people are coming to agree that a government's deliberate killing of one of its citizens is barbaric.

Traditionalist: And yet a great many people still believe that a murderer should forfeit not only his freedom, but for the most vicious killings his life.

A: Not so many think that anymore, apparently.

T: Executions have become unusual, you have a point there. But that is mainly because some lawyers and judges have been acting as legal saboteurs for decades, endlessly re-litigating each capital case. Juries, however, when confronted with the circumstances of wanton and savage murders, especially multiple murders, often enough call for the ultimate penalty.

A: They would repent their decision if they had witnessed an execution, or if they could imagine one vividly.

T: How vivid is your imagination of the horror of a cold-blooded murder? How many families or friends of those tortured and slain have you tried to console?

A: Vengeance is a sorry excuse for the perpetration of new cruelties.

T: You would deny a shattered and bereaved family the satisfaction of seeing the murderer suitably punished?

A: A murderer can be quite suitably punished by life imprisonment.

T: Juries are generally given that leeway, and they often use it where the circumstances make the crime at least a little less shocking. Where that is not the case, however, justice can demand more.

A: Even the most vicious and depraved murderers do not really earn their own murder. Bloodthirstiness has no proper part to play in justice.

T: A carefully informed determination that a murderer should die usually causes a jury real anguish. There is nothing feral or primitive involved.

A: None of us can know with certainty that anyone really deserves to forfeit his life.

T: We sometimes need to act decisively despite the possibility of error. Official vacillation in the face of true evil is grossly irresponsible.

A: Our first responsibility is to prevent a mistaken execution, which is fatal and irreversible. Error here is a deadly poison injected into the moral bloodstream of society.

T: Official fecklessness in the face of an atrocity is even more poisonous. Perfect and error-free justice is a fantasy, a utopian dream — where fantasies belong.

A: The substitution of life imprisonment for judicial execution is not going to paralyze any legal system.

T: Probably not. But don't you think that a man tempted to kill someone, if he fears for his own life, might shrink from destroying another's?

A: You cannot prove that even one homicide was ever prevented by that fear.

T: The assertion that no homicide ever was prevented by that fear is not only unprovable, it is hardly even credible. The amount of cruelty suffered, overall, is very likely diminished when the law allows the ultimate retribution for the most terrible crimes.

A: Trying to weigh and measure different cruelties, tit-for-tat, is futile. It's a distraction. There are certain deeds so plainly and incontrovertibly wrong that they can never be justified, no matter what the purpose or the circumstances. A civilized government's cold-blooded killing of one of its own citizens is a prime example.

T: Suppose the democratic Weimar Republic of Germany had executed Adolf Hitler in the 1920s, for his leadership of an attempted putsch. Would that have been wrong?

A: If you have to search a hundred years of world history to come up with a plausible example, that's a pretty good sign that the principle you are defending is not really defensible.

T: Search world history? The voices of the many millions whom Hitler eventually sent to their deaths do not sound even faintly in your ears? You simply aren't interested in the broader consequences of judicial execution?

A: The consequences of judicial executions are numerous, no doubt, and surely ambiguous. But your speculations about them, or anyone's, are beside the point.

T: I don't see why your speculations are any more to the point. You do agree, I assume, that even the best governments must sometimes be prepared to kill. War, for example, may require killing in defense of a nation's safety and independence.

A: That is a different problem entirely.

T: Why so? Aren't lethal crimes a kind of small-scale war on society?

A: Modern governments have available more sophisticated and more humane methods of deterring crime. They can meet their responsibilities without the hangman's noose.

T: And without concerning themselves overly much about higher murder rates? The question you keep trying to evade is whether modern governments can best protect the lives of all their citizens by keeping available the option of putting to death — carefully and humanely of course — those few who prove themselves a real threat to the lives of others.

A: These sorts of arguments are interminable. But I see the day coming when courts will renounce the savage practice you are trying to defend. Judges and attorneys have to grapple with its inconsistencies and its horrors at first hand, year after year. Many of them are longing to be done with the loathsome business.

T: The judges might decide to join you in your leap of faith. Are you asking them to rely upon their personal intuition? Will some sort of revelation come their way? Are you praying for divine intervention?

A: It pleases you to joke about this? The more we learn about a problem, the sounder our moral judgments become. The lawyers and the judges, the ones intimately involved in death penalty cases, need to go ahead and do what they know is right.

T: I'm not joking, I'm asking why you claim some sort of infallible moral insight without having shown any right to it. And your personal presumption is matched by your political irresponsibility. You hold the judgment of millions of your fellow citizens in contempt. Enough, you say, the experts will tell us what progress requires, and then everyone's duty will be to salute and march after them in formation. So much for the quaint idea of self-government.

Who will reconcile these two? Or, who will prove that one of them is plainly correct, the other simply mistaken?

No one, it seems safe to say.

* * *

There is a somewhat different approach we might have looked for from the abolitionist:

A: Every human life is sacred.

Perhaps he did say that, in an oblique way. A little reflection, however, may persuade us that he had good reason not to use that wording. So simple a statement on his part would have invited an equally simple rebuttal from the traditionalist:

T: That is exactly my point.

And with this, the two would seem to have entangled themselves again, unproductively, in a statistical analysis of homicide rates. But the question is not only about numbers. It is also about the idea of moral hazard — to what extent legal incentives improve or degrade behavior. It is a question of psychology.

More broadly, it is a question about human nature. The word "sacred" bears religious connotations.

American judges think of themselves as secular officials. The Supreme Court has gone so far as to declare that the Constitution must be interpreted in a religiously neutral manner. Arguments as to what is sacred and what is profane are not welcome at the Court. If judges reasoning in these terms attempted to award a final and comprehensive legal victory to one side or the other in the death penalty debate, they would invite accusations, quite plausible accusations, that they were promulgating religious legislation. It is an awkwardness for the American legal system that three of the formative dimensions of human life — the moral, the cultural, and the religious — must necessarily be touched by any general verdict, yea or nay, on the death penalty. Such a verdict, should one emerge, might come about through a legal decision; but if so that will be no ordinary legal decision.

This should be a little disconcerting, should it not, to good citizens of the United States of America? Our courts are not supposed to be all-purpose moral authorities. They were assigned a less ambitious purpose, that of interpreting and applying general laws to particular cases. Even less have American judges been appointed superintendents of American culture. Least of all, we hope, do many Americans credit judges with some rare and extraordinary spiritual insight. Our traditions teach us a healthy suspicion toward governmental officials, not an automatic or habitual deference.

And yet, there is a second fact which must be set alongside the quasi-religious character of the decision confronted by nine Supreme Court Justices in 1976. The request then made to the Court, for a ruling abolishing the death penalty, had at least a plausible textual basis in the Eighth Amendment to the nation's Constitution:

> Excessive bail shall not be required, nor excessive fines imposed, nor cruel and unusual punishments inflicted.

With that final phrase, all the considerations outlined above, moral, cultural, and spiritual, became a part of the criminal law of the United States. The Justices of the 1970s were stretching their jurisdiction little, if at all, when they considered whether to abolish capital punishment. Nor, apparently, would Congress be obviously exceeding its powers, should it decide to take up the issue.

* * *

Then again, another uncomfortable fact requires our attention, alongside the cultural gravity of the 1976 case and the Constitution's seeming invitation to the Justices to resolve that case. Most Americans, for a long time, have considered themselves committed to a separation between church and state. The Justices and other prominent American leaders have endorsed that ideal and have sought to give it legal effect. Yet a condemnation of unnecessary cruelty, a theme quite admirably fit for a minister's sermon, appears in the Bill of Rights.

That is to say: The Eighth Amendment could be, at least potentially, at cross-purposes with the opening words of the First Amendment: "Congress shall make no law respecting an establishment of religion, or prohibiting the free exercise thereof;..." The Eighth Amendment could be understood to authorize a legal definition, narrow but quite important, of cruelty. Such a definition, if promulgated, would establish a highly ambiguous but culturally potent mandate for mercy, or for compassion. The resulting law would be hard to distinguish from a doctrinal pronouncement issuing out of Jerusalem, or out of Rome.

Did the statesmen of Philadelphia suffer a momentary lapse of attention or judgment in 1791 when the Bill of Rights became effective?

We would be rash to assume so. We would do better to wonder whether we are still good readers of our founding political documents. We need to question an all-too-easy but quite careless assumption: that the separation of church from state means, or accomplishes, the separation of religion from politics. We should allow that the disentanglement of religion and politics, if such an ambition is realizable at all, may be much more complicated than we would like to assume. A national orthodoxy as to the legitimacy of capital punishment, should one be created, would hardly be the work of some particular church, nor even of many churches working together. Indeed, it might well run contrary to the religious views of numerous sects and denominations. That orthodoxy, nonetheless, would wear every appearance of a religious doctrine.

We need to recognize that the American founders may well have thought more carefully and more soundly about these matters than their political posterity. For we have now seen, in the twentieth century and since, the interrelations between American law, morality, culture, and religion become very confused, very complicated, and often very bitter. Much of that confusion and complication, moreover, has arisen out of the work of our latter-day Supreme Court Justices. The reader will probably have little difficulty citing instances in which the Justices have acted quite forthrightly as cultural therapists to the American nation, or as a committee for general cultural improvement.

In this small book I examine a selection of significant Supreme Court rulings, looking at them not with a lawyer's concerns only, but from the broader perspectives outlined above. I seek to illuminate some of the ways by which a constitutional Court has transformed itself into a cultural magisterium.

And, I hope to persuade the reader that the Court ought to renounce that exalted ambition.

CHAPTER ONE: CELEBRATION

Polygamy was a crime throughout the early United States: an antique form of marriage encountered in the pages of the Old Testament, but definitely not one to be condoned in the New World. Nonetheless there must have been stories about it, perhaps even instances of it, among the American colonists and in the newly independent nation; for people are unlikely to criminalize what they never see or hear or worry about. The consensus was disturbed in the early nineteenth century, however, when an American prophet, Joseph Smith, founder of the Mormon faith, set an example for his followers by taking several wives.

The open celebration of such marriages, with their large households and extensive networks of kinship, provoked a sharp and indignant reaction in the communities most directly affected. The resulting hostility, to polygamy and to the beleaguered Mormons more generally, drove the new sect from place to place. Finally, far westward across the continent in sparsely populated Utah, they found by mid-century isolation enough to enjoy some peace and security.

So, for a time, Mormons did not much trouble their fellow citizens. As residents of an American territory, they were allowed a measure of local self-government. The distant convulsions of the Civil War and its aftermath spared them the close attention of their countrymen. But polygamy was a crime under the Congressional enactments which governed Utah; and in 1878 a Mormon bigamist, convicted and sentenced by a territorial court, fought back. Pleading his right to religious liberty, he appealed to the nation's highest court.

His plea, the Mormons' plea, fell on deaf ears. The arguments that Mormons offered in behalf of their law of marriage were no more persuasive to the Supreme Court than they had been to Congress. The unanimous Justices saw nothing morally or legally questionable about mandatory monogamy.[2]

The prosecutions continued, and were supplemented in the 1880s with institutional suppression — the confiscation of Mormon houses of worship. The Supreme Court approved these measures in 1890.[3] Finally, with their leaders driven into hiding and their churches closed, the Mormons capitulated. As soon as they conformed their law to the prevailing marital orthodoxy, however, their properties were returned and the repression ended. Statehood for Utah followed shortly.

* * *

Early in the twenty-first century the Supreme Court was presented again with a controversy as to the nature of the marital relation. In 2015, five Justices startled many Americans with a legal innovation. They expanded the definition of marriage, nationwide, to include unions between persons of the same sex; a change which, although already initiated by a number of state governments, still faced strong opposition in other states.[4]

These two judicial treatments of the law of marriage, widely separated in time, also differed markedly in their style and their thinking. They may seem to have little in common but their subject matter. Nonetheless, that is an invitation to comparison, for marriage is a very important institution. Marriage is the basis for families, and in family settings occur the earliest and most formative influences upon the attitudes and characters of rising generations. A culture may be said, with little

---

[2] Reynolds v. United States, 250 U.S. 104 (1878)
[3] Mormon Church v. United States, 136 U.S. 1 (1890)
[4] Obergefell v. Hodges, docket number 14-556 (2015)

exaggeration, to be grounded in the families which comprise its smallest social units and the nurseries of its children. Changes in the law of marriage are seldom taken lightly; and those who would compel such change have a question to answer: By what right?

That is a question which, in the United States, points to the nation's Constitution.

Note, however, before beginning such an inquiry, a preliminary observation. The word "marriage" does not appear in the Constitution. How much, then, can this short document, a few thousand words of very general principles and directives, really have to say on the subject?

Be that as it may, we can begin by reviewing what those involved in litigating the law of marriage in 1878, and in 2015, thought that the Constitution has to say — or, perhaps, what the Constitution has no need to say.

*   *   *

The nineteenth century struggle over American polygamy began in the courts and legislatures of the states where the Mormon sect arose and grew. From those regional settings, the fight then moved into Congress. At some point Congress prohibited polygamy in the Utah Territory, setting the stage for the 1878 litigation. No one at the time questioned the right of local governments to address the topic. Thoughtful Americans of that time might well have questioned the propriety of Congressmen doing so; yet, there was some support for the national legislation in the text of the Constitution.

For one thing: In territories of the United States, as distinguished from states, Article IV Section 3 empowers Congress to make "all needful rules and regulations." This is broad language. Although the enumeration of Congressional responsibilities appearing in Article I Section 8 does not include the laws of marriage, it is not clear that Congressional authority must stop short of that subject in a territory which may later join the Union as a state.

In addition: Article IV Section 4 directs the United States to guarantee to "every State in this Union a Republican Form of

Government." A polygamous family, in the nineteenth century, was fairly described as a patriarchal family. Further, it is at least plausible, and it was argued by nineteenth century politicians and judges, that patriarchy encourages a more hierarchical social order. If so, polygamous marriages at that time might well have worked against the egalitarian principles and institutions of self-government, bringing Article IV Section 4 into play.

These two provisions of the Constitution do not directly address the topic of marriage. They do not prescribe monogamy as the law of the land. Arguably, however, they might encompass Congressional regulation of marriage practices within a territory of the United States. We cannot say, therefore, that Congress obviously exceeded its authority in criminalizing polygamous marriages in Utah. And, with that legislation promulgated and challenged, it then became the duty of the Supreme Court to assess the constitutional propriety of the contested statute.

The Court of 1878, in other words, had a sound basis for its involvement in the struggle over polygamy. That conclusion stops short, of course, of the central legal question: Does the Constitution allow Congress to prohibit polygamy within a territory of the United States?

Two constitutional provisions tending to support the Congressional prohibition have been noted. What, on the other hand, might be found in the Constitution tending the other way? What might we find that would seem to support the Mormon law of marriage as a legitimate exercise of local political authority?

The Mormons cited the opening of the First Amendment:

> Congress shall make no law respecting an establishment of religion, or prohibiting the free exercise thereof; or abridging the freedom of speech, or of the press, or the right of the people peaceably to assemble, and to petition the Government for a redress of grievances.

They accused the Congress, that is, of impermissibly abridging their religious rights as American citizens. And indeed, if the Mormon law of marriage is conceded to be a religious law, the question becomes unavoidable: What would authorize Congress to nullify it? The Justices of 1878 avoided the issue by simply denying that monogamy has anything to do with religion. That sufficed to avoid also the related question whether Congress had, in effect, established monogamy as a mandatory article of religious practice, if not of religious faith.

The Mormons could also have made of Article IV Section 4, the guarantee of republican government, a double-edged sword. Against the argument that polygamy promotes an anti-republican social and political hierarchy, they could have pointed out that the citizenry of Utah, including its women, had given no evidence of significant opposition to polygamy. For the Mormon leaders, concerned about the accusation that they were imposing a deviant form of marriage upon a reluctant people, had enfranchised the women of the Territory in 1870, well before the movement for female suffrage had gained much traction nationwide. Mormons could have claimed credit for a major advance in republican principles, an advance which would require several decades to grow strong throughout the nation.

The Mormons could have strengthened both of these arguments by reminding the Justices of the omission of marriage law from the list of explicit Congressional responsibilities in Article I Section 8; an omission implying the reservation, to the local governments, of authority over the laws of the family.

Last, but far from least, the Mormons could have reminded the Justices of another pertinent constitutional provision, the Tenth Amendment to the Bill of Rights:

> The powers not delegated to the United States by the Constitution, nor prohibited by it to the States, are reserved to the States respectively, or to the people.

This Amendment speaks to the rights of local political communities vis-à-vis the central government of the United States. The Mormons were such a community. They were politically organized under a territorial government, and they were actively asserting their authority over a topic not expressly delegated by the Constitution to the central government.

How much, then, should the policy favoring local political authority, embodied in the Tenth Amendment, corroborate and strengthen the policy of religious pluralism implicit in the First Amendment? Should these two important Amendments, taken together, outweigh the more general provisions of Article IV, Sections 3 and 4? Why, despite the directives of the First and Tenth Amendments, should American citizens residing in a territory have to wait until statehood to enjoy the fundamental rights of local self-government and religious liberty?

These were the kinds of questions that lawyers and judges, doing their specialized jobs carefully, needed to engage in 1878. So far as the case report discloses, however, only one of those questions was actually engaged, and only by one side of the controversy. Lawyers for the Mormons claimed the protection of the First Amendment, whereupon the Justices went through the motions of responding. But the Justices responded only in the most cursory and superficial terms; rather, they contented themselves with pouring scorn upon the Mormon law of marriage.

Altogether this appears to have been an unprofessional performance on the part of the lawyers involved. No less than six pertinent constitutional provisions invited vigorous debate, pro and con. Even with the case so poorly developed, however, we cannot say that the Court's ruling was simply wrong. It was neither clearly erroneous nor clearly valid. The Constitution, silent on the topic of marriage, left too much ambiguity for a truly compelling legal decision.

* * *

Turning, then, to the later ruling: What constitutional text, if any, might support the Supreme Court's expansion of marriage in 2015 to include homosexual unions?

The five Justices making up the majority sought justification in the Fourteenth Amendment:

> No State shall make or enforce any law which shall abridge the privileges or immunities of citizens of the

United States; nor shall any State deprive any person of life, liberty, or property without due process of law; nor deny to any person within its jurisdiction the equal protection of the laws.

But this simply will not do. No philosophy of marriage can be plausibly derived from abstract phrases such as due process of law, or equal protection of the laws, or privileges and immunities. No science of sexuality can be found there. The Amendment expresses a strong but partial understanding of human nature and human flourishing. The vision it articulates surely yields some general and very important principles; but still it is a legal vision, narrow enough to accommodate quite different marital codes. The Fourteenth Amendment cannot, by itself, yield the mandate issued by the majority Justices in 2015. And the fact that it could not was evident from their written opinion. For they had recourse to arguments reaching far beyond the scope of the Amendment.

Concerning the importance of marriage, they spoke of its transcendence; of its status as a keystone of the social order; of its vital purpose of promoting a way of life.

They spoke of the most basic human needs, the deepest hopes, the most profound aspirations.

They spoke of new dimensions of freedom, to be discerned in the ongoing quest for individual autonomy and dignity.

What inspiring words, what lofty ideas! But they do not appear in the Constitution of the United States, and there is a reason for that. From the rhetoric of progress, let alone from the poetry of transcendence, there is no straight line to legal rules. Judicial propriety required the Justices' to bend their path to homosexual marriage through the Constitution; but they bent the Constitution in doing so. No more convincing was their bow of respect to democratic process, even as they decreed that as of 2015 democracy had sufficiently run its course on the question before them.

Eleven out of fifty local governments had by then already legitimized same-sex marriage. Officials in these states, presumably with the support of the citizens they represented, had thought about the meaning of transcendence, of basic human needs, of profound hopes and aspirations, of freedom, of autonomy, of dignity. They had applied their conclusions to the topic of marriage, and provided a new civic sacrament supplementing the traditional marriage rites. Some other local governments had created what they called civil unions for the same purpose; but still declined to celebrate those novel marriages with the traditional name, a name rich in historical and cultural connotations. In several regions of the nation, however, marital tradition remained too powerful even for the half-way measure.

* * *

Neither the Justices of 1878, nor those of the majority in 2015, interrogated the constitutional text in any serious way. In the 1870s and 1880s they were preoccupied to the verge of obsession with the scandal of polygamy. The proprieties of their office made no appearance in the following typical passage:

> Bigamy and polygamy are crimes by the law of all civilized and Christian countries. They are crimes by the laws of the United States ... They tend to destroy the purity of the marriage relation, to disturb the peace of the family, to degrade woman, and to debase man. Few crimes are more pernicious to the best interests of society, and receive more general or more deserved punishment. To extend exemption from punishment for such crimes would be to shock the moral judgment of the community. To call their advocacy a tenet of religion is to offend the common sense of mankind.[5]

Here the nineteenth century Justices, their ire quite displacing their judicial demeanor, used language more suited to a minister's sermon than a judge's legal reasoning. Accusing Mormons of personal debasement and religious fraud, the Court joined the Congress on crusade. Both institutions made abundantly clear their determination to force an American religious

---

[5] Davis v. Beason, 133 U.S. 333 (1890)

sect into the surrender of a way of life they considered divinely blessed.

In 2015, the majority Justices disclosed their real concerns almost as clearly. Five Justices, in 2015, summoned their fellow citizens to new exertions of grace and charity. They envisioned a new beatitude, and catechized the American nation in it. They too preached a sermon, one framed by very different ideas and expressed in quite different terms: a twenty-first century sermon rather than a nineteenth century.

The nineteenth-century Justices reinforced an existing civic sacrament with official curses upon what they regarded as a profane heresy. The twenty-first century Justices established a new and mandatory civic sacrament in which the idea of marriage is shorn of its traditional association with physical complementarity and procreative purpose.

The persecution suffered by the Mormons in the late nineteenth century was blatant and forceful. The persecution embodied in the Court's decision in 2015 was oblique and subtle. The Justices of 2015 confiscated a privilege traditionally belonging to American citizens: the privilege of determining what forms of marriage are to be celebrated, what forms merely recognized, and what forms officially considered profane. In 2015 the American people suffered a diminution of their constitutional immunity to factional politics, a politics of edicts lacking broad electoral support.

Let us turn next to the question of persecution.

CHAPTER TWO: PERSECUTION

As the Second World War approached, a local school board in Pennsylvania decided to require in its classrooms a daily recital of the pledge of allegiance to the United States. Some pupils, however, would not comply; for their families, members of a small but very earnest Christian group, considered the pledge a forbidden act of idolatry. When the recusant children were expelled for defiance, their parents sued the school district. They asked that their religious convictions be accommodated. They also complained of the expense of private schooling, a burden which most other citizens of the State were spared.

Their suit reached the Supreme Court, where eight Justices, in 1940, allowed this educational policy to stand.[6] The request for religious exemption from a generally applicable civic duty, they observed, was not favored in American law. They emphasized the importance of cultivating patriotism among the young, and of the flag as a symbol of national unity. They noted that allowing religious dissent in so light a matter as a brief and perfunctory ritual of the school morning would require them to reverse several earlier decisions. And they worried that they were being asked to act as a legislature.

In the aftermath of this decision the legislature of another state, West Virginia, adopted a similar policy in its schools,

---

[6] Minersville School District v. Gobitis, 310 U.S. 586 (1940)

which promptly brought forth a similar lawsuit; and in 1943 the Supreme Court reversed the precedent it had set three years earlier. Six Justices — three of whom had voted in favor of the earlier decision — now condemned the mandatory pledge as compelled speech, as a coerced expression of beliefs not held or attitudes not shared. Neither the speech itself, they argued, nor the omission of it, threatened any harm or abridged the rights of any other individual. Such compulsion, they said, the Constitution does not permit.[7]

* * *

Now let us become time travelers, moving forward some eight decades. The setting is Colorado, where the owner of a small bakery refused to provide a wedding cake for a homosexual marriage ceremony. Brought by his offended customers before his state's civil rights commission, he was ordered to change his policies; and he and his employees were summoned to training sessions in tolerance. His protest — that his religious convictions did not permit him to participate in such ceremonies — was rejected, and he was accused of bigotry and illegal discrimination.

The baker's case also made its way to the nation's Supreme Court, where in 2018 five Justices nullified his punishment.[8]

* * *

But what have wedding cakes to do with the Pledge of Allegiance?

Each of these three suits challenged a state or municipal law.

Each suit originated in a similar pattern of conflict. Each involved an invitation to join in celebrating something — the nation, or a wedding — an invitation which, when declined, became a demand.

Another obvious link: Each refusal was religiously motivated.

Each case, therefore, poses the following questions. Under what circumstances may one who will not, on grounds of

[7] Barnette v. West Virginia Board of Education, 319 U.S. 624 (1943)
[8] Masterpiece Cakeshop v. Colorado Civil Rights Commission, docket number 16-111 (2018)

conscience, participate in a ceremony, be punished? What public interest, if any, might support a local government's concern with a citizen's decision, for religious reasons, not to affirm some belief or some public policy?

The penalties imposed here, by historical standards, were mild: the denial of access to a basic education at taxpayer expense, on the one hand; on the other, submission to compulsory indoctrination — to a show of confessing sin and vowing repentance. Relatively lenient as these punishments may have been, however, they were burdensome and humiliating. These supposed miscreants were officially and publicly shamed.

In a word: They were persecuted, albeit in a very civil manner.

* * *

What do we find in the Constitution bearing upon the authority of local governments to require ceremonial observances, and to punish delinquents?

A review of the constitutional text turns up several pertinent provisions. The most specific is found in Article VI:

> The Senators and Representatives before mentioned, and the Members of the several State Legislatures, and all executive and judicial Officers, both of the United States and of the several States, shall be bound by Oath or Affirmation, to support this Constitution; but no religious Test shall ever by required as a Qualification to any Office or public Trust under the United States.

Here the authors of the Philadelphia Constitution required all American public officials, state and national, to swear loyalty to that charter. They exempted officials of the central government from religious tests — but they conspicuously did not exempt state or municipal officials. Nothing in Article VI limited the authority of local governments to require oaths, either of their officers or their citizens. And since several states of the early Republic maintained religious establishments, we may be sure that American citizens sometimes found their legal status affected by their willingness to comply.

Article VI, then, set within its historical context, rebuts the idea put forth by the majority Justices in 1943 — that the compulsory utterance of some affirmation necessarily violates the spirit of the Constitution.

And the bearing of Article VI upon the case of the baker? Its application here depends upon an analogy; quite a reasonable analogy, however. The baker was pressed to make his services available to the complaining customer and to acknowledge an obligation to serve similar customers in the future; thereby publicly endorsing the sexual morality which his state government had blessed and was supporting with legal protections. With appropriate words and actions — with an oath, so to speak — he could have averted his persecution.

As to all three of these cases, then, Article VI, with its prominent omission, suggests that there should be considerable latitude allowed the local governments regarding these sensitive concerns.

* * *

And beyond Article VI? As always, where religion is involved, we must consider the First Amendment:

> Congress shall make no law respecting an establishment of religion, or prohibiting the free exercise thereof; or abridging the freedom of speech, or of the press, or the right of the people peaceably to assemble, and to petition the government for a redress of grievances.

The protesting schoolchildren and parents were being penalized for their public expression of unpopular religious convictions. They had dared to offend a politically powerful group of their fellow citizens. Similarly, the baker complained that his state government was compelling his artistic participation in a ceremony he considered religiously profane.

But if the local governments could properly require a religious oath of public officers, why could they not require a similar oath of their citizens? If local governments could properly do this, then, it seems, the First Amendment was not intended to encompass each and every exercise of religious conviction. To read that Amendment as negating an authority left with the states by Article VI of the constitutional text would be to place two distinct constitutional provisions, written within four years of one another, in conflict. This is not to be done casually or carelessly.

Perhaps, however, some later Amendment might have altered the balance between Article VI and the First Amendment? As was usual by the 1940s and since, the Justices, in cases such as these, also relied upon the Fourteenth Amendment:

> No State shall make or enforce any law which shall abridge the privileges or immunities of citizens of the United States; nor shall any State deprive any person of life, liberty, or property, without due process of law; nor deny to any person within its jurisdiction the equal protection of the laws.

Supposing there is a conflict between Article VI of the constitutional text and the First Amendment — which is not at all clear, since the latter only refers to Congress, not to the state governments — might the Fourteenth Amendment be understood to have nationalized the law of oaths and affirmations, thereby superseding (after seventy-seven years) a historical prerogative of American local governments?

In other words: Should we understand the Fourteenth Amendment to have created a new privilege of American citizens, exempting them from oaths and affirmations which might otherwise have been required by their state or municipality?

Perhaps. But where the Constitution expressly provides more leeway for the local governments — as it plainly did in Article VI and in the First Amendment — the balance of considerations may well run against uniformity, against the principle of one rule for all. The constitutional text calls for a holistic reading. A few of its words, or a provision or two, often will not provide clear guidance.

A holistic reading, in fact, quickly turns up another requirement pertinent to the cases under discussion here. The idea of equal protection under the laws, another mandate of the

Fourteenth Amendment, had real purchase upon two of these controversies. The protesting schoolchildren and parents were being denied equal access to a valuable public benefit, education, made generally available by their state government; and in one case they expressly complained of that burden. This kind of legal distinction was targeted in 1868 for review at the national level.

Yet the Justices of the 1940s were so focused upon the religious question that they paid no attention to this other issue. That said, we need to acknowledge that no real clarity would have emerged had they done so. An alleged denial of equal protection by state laws was the subject of so many judicial reviews that the Court developed, early on, a formulaic response: In general, a local government may treat one class of its citizens differently from another when the difference is reasonably related to a proper public purpose.

Under this approach, the 1940 Court considered the mandatory pledge of allegiance a reasonable means of cultivating patriotism, a proper governmental purpose. The 1943 Court disagreed. But with this impasse we have arrived at the sort of controversy which turns as much or more upon the differing commitments and sensibilities of different judges, as upon any reasoning that they bring to bear.

* * *

Once more, having considered the most relevant constitutional provisions, we find our specific question unresolved. Once again, we need to interrogate the text for more general, but still relevant passages. And again, doing so, we easily find several.

There is the Tenth Amendment:

> The powers not delegated to the United States by the Constitution, nor prohibited by it to the States, are reserved to the States respectively, or to the people.

This speaks directly to the problem of resolving constitutional ambiguities. It instructs the nation's government, other things being equal, to leave at the local level those powers and responsibilities that the constitutional authors decided to leave there.

There is, as well, Article IV Section 4, which obligates the nation to guarantee to each state a republican form of government. This should create a strong presumption against the nullification of local legislation either by Congress or by the Supreme Court.

Nor should we omit Section 5 of the Fourteenth Amendment. When the Justices, citing this Amendment, decide to nullify a state law, they need to explain why they are ignoring its final section, which assigns responsibility for enforcement to Congress. Rarely do they offer any explanation. They offered none in 1943, nor again in 2018.

Not to be omitted in this regard, moreover, are the important constitutional silences. Article I Section 8, where the responsibilities and authorities of Congress are specified, makes no reference to schooling or education; nor any reference to sexual morality. If the nation's legislature may not specify an opening ceremony for the school day, or prohibit one, why should the nation's courts presume to exercise that authority? If the nation's legislature is not to concern itself with the law of marriage, if marriage is classified by the Constitution as a local concern, what gives the nation's judiciary jurisdiction over a wedding dispute?

* * *

To sum up: The most directly pertinent constitutional provisions offer no compelling demonstration of the validity of any of these three constitutional rulings.

The Justices who decided the 1940 case had the weight of tradition and precedent on their side. Still, one Justice argued strenuously — and not unpersuasively, as became evident three years later — for a different reading of the nation's fundamental charter.

In both 1943 and 2018, several general provisions of the Constitution suggest quite persuasively that the Court was intruding improperly into the realm of local law and politics.

Are these constitutional conclusions debatable? Surely so. But to become caught up in debating them, and to go no further, is to miss the larger dimensions of the conflicts out of which the decisions arose. The critic who remains within the lawyer's professional horizon may easily overlook an unspoken assumption.

The Justices who decided these cases assumed, in effect, that the lawyer's perspective sufficed to frame an adequate exploration of the character and the implications of their decision. One Justice, in 1940, was clearly uncomfortable with the ongoing erosion of local prerogatives. Eight of them held firm at that time against the gathering pressures toward centralization and conformity. Among those eight Justices, however, several apparently were wavering. Several changed their minds in 1943. None of the Justices, early or late, expressed any concern about the longer term. None worried about the consequences of having a single unelected authority supervising persecutions throughout a vast and populous nation. No Justice seemed to recognize that the power to decide, on such a scale, what may or may not be persecuted, is the power to give form and direction to an entire culture.

* * *

Cultures and religions are intertwined and inseparable. The Justices of 1940, as they expressed themselves in the Constitution's language of civic accommodation, were also showing tolerance for political and religious pluralism. By 1943 they were changing the nature of American tolerance: toward individual privilege, away from community prerogative. And by 2018 the Court's acceptance of cultural and religious diversity had eroded a good deal further.

Indeed, the Court's accelerating quest for uniformity had been dramatically illustrated in 2015, when five Justices, on their own authority, decreed an important change in the law of marriage throughout the United States.[9]

---

[9] Obergefell v. Hodges, docket number 14-556 (2015)

Approval or disapproval; encouragement or discouragement; praise or blame; assistance or obstruction; and, most emphatically, celebration or persecution. By means of these attitudes and actions, a culture, over time, maintains itself, reproduces itself — and changes. Cultures evolve. Those who attain cultural leadership, who can set the terms of celebration and persecution, hold two very important keys to the future. With those keys in hand they can strongly influence, if not fully control, the pace and the direction of cultural change.

Magistrates so powerful, moreover, may be tempted to add a third key to their collection. They may aspire to an even larger role in the shaping or reshaping of their culture. They may decide that they need to school coming generations regarding truth and falsehood, good and evil, nobility and ignominy.

Next let us watch the Justices of the Supreme Court reaching, in several instances, for that third key.

CHAPTER THREE: ACCULTURATION

By the twentieth century, in the United States, public schools provided most education at the elementary and secondary levels. There were thousands of school districts. Each was a small governmental agency, locally organized and administered pursuant to statutes of the state in which it was located. Each had the power to tax within its boundaries. Each was supervised by a board of citizens residing within the district and elected by their fellow residents. Each offered practically cost-free basic education to children and adolescents within a certain geographical area. Each had substantial authority over the content and character of its teaching; and collectively, they reflected the considerable variety to be encountered across a nation of continental extent. Numerous, heterogeneous, relatively self-governing, together the schools operated by these districts provided most Americans their first schooling, and many Americans their only schooling.

Not all Americans, however. Throughout the nation there remained a great many private schools. These were funded and operated by the parents whose children attended them; or, very frequently, by parents in partnership with a church or synagogue.

During the course of the twentieth century, the nation's Supreme Court began to issue rulings which shaped or reshaped relations between public schools, private schools, and religious organizations. Three of these cases will be the focus here.

* * *

In 1922 the government of one state, Oregon, decided to make its public schools mandatory for all residents. Whatever the motives, this novel policy represented an aggressive challenge to a long tradition of parental prerogative. So bold an innova-tion could hardly have been expected, in the United States, to escape litigation. This one did not. Without delay, the Society of the Sisters of the Holy Names of Jesus and Mary, fighting the attempt to empty their school of students, sought protection in the courts of the nation.

And indeed, when the case reached the Supreme Court in 1925, the Justices held the Oregon law unconstitutional.[10] The ruling put Americans on notice that no local government would be allowed a legal monopoly over the education of the young.

* * *

A little over two decades later, in 1948, the Court took another opportunity to consider the interaction of religious institutions and the public schools. This time the Justices decided that local decisions about curriculum can bear constitutional significance.

The school district which was the focus of the Justices' atten-tion was providing, in cooperation with a citizen group repre-senting the Protestant, Catholic, and Jewish faiths, very brief but regular sessions of religious instruction. Once each week, for thirty or forty-five minutes depending upon age, pupils whose parents requested participation were instructed by a minister, a priest, or a rabbi. These visiting teachers were selected and paid by a church or synagogue, but had to be approved by the public school superintendent. Pupils whose parents did not wish them to attend did not, and were provided alternative instruction or supervision.

Programs like this, designed to supplement an education in arts and sciences and history, were not unusual at the time. Nonetheless, eight Justices declared the practice unconstitu-

---

[10] Pierce v. Society of Sisters, 268 U.S. 510 (1925)

tional on the grounds that it unacceptably entangled church and state.[11]

* * *

Next, with the passage of another decade or so, brief ceremonial prayers offered at the opening of the school day became a point of contention. A great many Americans supported the practice. Some did not, however, objecting that students at taxpayer-supported schools should encounter there no official promotion of any religious views or practices.

In 1962 the Supreme Court took up the question. The Justices held that the following short prayer, composed by a state agency for recital in elementary and secondary schools, represented another impermissible entanglement of church and state:

> Almighty God, we acknowledge our dependence upon Thee, and we beg Thy blessings upon us, our parents, our teachers, and our country.

These few words surely represented a modest theism, we might almost say a vestigial theism. Here we find no account of creation, no founder or messiah or blessed one, no narrative of salvation, no vision of the world to come, no stern moral commandments, no modes of worship, no mandatory rites or disciplines. The God so addressed might seem to have withdrawn from the scene of human affairs. This twenty-two word devotional was the outcome of efforts at the lower levels of American government to find an acceptable compromise between American theists and American secularists.

But compromise on this very sensitive topic held no appeal for six Justices in 1962.[12]

* * *

Readers looking back today at the earliest of these three decisions may be surprised to find the Court ignoring the First Amendment. Those who know a little constitutional history will not be puzzled, however; for the historical First Amend-

---

[11] McCollum v. Board of Education, 333 U.S. 203 (1948)
[12] Engel v. Vitale, 370 U.S. 421 (1962)

ment, the literal First Amendment, gave the nation no authority over local religious policies or legislation. The Justices, at the time of the 1925 controversy, still observed that limitation. Despite their hostility toward Oregon's educational high-handedness, they found in the Bill of Rights, as traditionally understood, no help. They were not at a loss — they found a way to preserve the right of parents to send their children to a church school rather than a public school; but they spoke not at all about religion. They resorted to abstractions and circumlocutions. They spoke about business corporations, about property rights, about personal liberty. They spoke about reasonableness versus unreasonableness, a distinction sometimes helpful but more often merely a tacit agreement to disagree.

The two later cases were deliberated under the First Amendment. Or, to speak precisely, those cases were deliberated under a reinterpreted First Amendment. The Justices' new First Amendment reads thus:

> Neither Congress nor any state government shall make any law respecting an establishment of religion, or prohibiting the free exercise thereof; or abridging the freedom of speech, or of the press, or the right of the people peaceably to assemble, and to petition the Government for a redress of grievances.

The reader has already encountered by this point the justification offered by the Court — the Fourteenth Amendment — for amending the First Amendment:

> No State shall make or enforce any law which shall abridge the privileges or immunities of citizens of the United States; nor shall any state deprive any person of life, liberty, or property, without due process of law; nor deny to any person within its jurisdiction the equal protection of the laws.

In this context, however — the banishment of clergy and prayer from public schools — it is fair to ask: How, specifically, did the silencing of religious voices in public places become a new privilege of American citizenship? When? What happened to the earlier privilege of speaking freely about religious faith, and of adjusting, through local governments, the interactions of civic and religious institutions?

Alternatively: Had a religious presence in a public school suddenly become a violation of due process of law? When? How? Why?

Or had the equal protection of the laws somehow begun to require the suppression of religious voices in public settings? When? How? Why?

To ask these questions is to see their oddity. To search the Justices' opinions for explanations is unavailing. What that search will turn up is a phrase, "separation of church and state," a phrase once uttered by a famous American; but a phrase lacking constitutional status and unaccompanied by any clear explanation of its meaning.

* * *

The oddities, moreover, are not limited to the Justices' handling of the First and Fourteenth Amendments. In all three of these school cases, they employed a good deal of creative lawyering. They did not canvass the entire constitutional text, asking what provision or provisions might argue against the decisions they handed down. They did not read the document as an integrated whole. They treated the Constitution as a collec-tion of sentences, from which they could select one or another on which to hang an argument.

Yet a holistic reading, had they made the effort, would not have left them without guidance.

There is Article I, which allocates the legislative powers of the national government to Congress. The same allocation appears in the final section of the Fourteenth Amendment itself, which charges Congress with the Amendment's enforcement. The bearing of religious concerns upon educational policies, throughout the life of the Republic, had been an uncontested prerogative of the local governments; so long uncontested as to acquire the force of customary law. Wasn't a sudden and important change in that law a legislative act, and therefore a Congressional responsibility?

Then there is Section 8 of Article I, the list of Congressional powers, which gives the new national legislature no authority over educational institutions or policies. If Congress could not properly do what the Court did in 1925 and 1948 and 1962, why should the Court be able to?

There is the Tenth Amendment, which reserved to the state governments and their citizens all powers neither delegated to the new central government nor prohibited to the states.

There is Article IV Section 4, which instructs Congress to guarantee to every state in the Union a republican form of government.

The Court's rulings in each of these three cases, striking down state legislation enacted in the political branches of local governments, look very much like authoritarian actions quite out of place in the American Republic.

* * *

The careful reader will note a certain tension to be seen in the tendencies of these judicial forays into the field of educational policy.

In 1925 the Court took a stand in favor of educational diversity. Governmental schooling in the United States, said the Justices, will be limited by the rights of parents. The cause of educational standardization should not be permitted to override the religious liberties of American citizens — in particular, the freedom of parents to see that their religious tradition plays an important role in the schooling of their children. "The child is not the mere creature of the state," said the Justices.

In the two later cases, however, the Court established two new orthodoxies to be observed in every governmental school throughout the United States.

No longer, in public classrooms, would clergy be allowed to provide any religious instruction whatever.

No longer, in public classrooms, could teachers lead students in even a brief and bland prayer.

These new orthodoxies, supposedly derived from the Constitution, were to be quite independent of any parental preference or influence. Children educated by the state, if they were not mere creatures of the state, seemed well on their way to becoming educational wards of the state.

The Justices did not speak in any of these cases about educational orthodoxies or, for that matter, about the rights of parents. They spoke as judges who were supposed to be keepers and interpreters of the nation's tablets. The Justices, as Justices, were not supposed to be representing any client other than the people of the United States. But in 1925 they seemed to be representing some of the people of the United States — those parents seeking a religiously-grounded education for their children. In 1948 and 1962 they seemed to be representing other parents, those who protested the appearance in their children's classrooms of any Christian or Jewish presence.

* * *

The larger point here, however, is not the Justices' insensitivity to the nature and constitutional proprieties of their office. The larger point is the character of the authority and responsibility that the Justices took upon themselves. In these three decisions we see the Court effectually declaring itself the final arbiter of educational policy in the United States. A little history can illuminate the meaning of this development.

Religion and education, in the West, had long been considered related and mutually supportive activities. Europe's universities were born within the cathedrals and monasteries of the Roman Church. One of a university's principal functions, well into the nineteenth century, was the training of a competent and learned clerisy to lead the churches and minister to the laity. In North America, from colonial times through the birth of the United States and beyond, this tradition continued. Religious and educational institutions often remained closely associated. Even in the first nation to invest with constitutional significance the distinction between what is Caesar's and what is God's, accommodations were usually found between American churches and schools.

The Justices' new pedagogy, however, was one in which the teaching of theism was to be eliminated. It was a pedagogy in which instruction as to the meaning and the history of theism might jeopardize an instructor's career. It was a pedagogy in which young Americans would no longer learn much about this subject. Young Americans, most of them, were henceforth to be raised up as citizens of a representative democracy, understanding their nation and their governance, fulfilling their responsibilities as citizens, without necessarily engaging the religious history of their culture, or encountering any committed, professing Christians or Jews.

There was great irony here, although it went generally unnoticed. The Justices were reviving a very old pedagogical practice and doctrine. In turning the central government of the United States into an educational authority — into something it had not been for its first one hundred and sixty years — they also, unwittingly, turned the American nation back toward an ancient religious tradition. The Justices re-entangled government and religion at the highest governmental level, the level where government and religion had been deliberately disentangled in 1787 and 1791. The Justices showed no awareness that their rulings — whether enabling or curtailing religious schooling — were themselves a form of religious legislation.

And yet the Justices, in issuing the two later rulings, claimed that they were separating church and state.

* * *

A people's history, a people's understanding of its history, is analogous to a person's memory. Memory shapes character in both individual and community. A substantial loss of memory can be depended upon to bring about a marked change in character, most probably a change for the worse. If theism remains a living tradition, with power to move peoples and to shape destinies, then the nation which averts its eyes from that fact chooses ignorance over knowledge. If theism is a living tradition — if, in its various forms, it inspires individuals and organizes vibrant communities — then all young persons, not only

Americans, have a compelling need to study its past, good and bad, and to become aware of its spiritual potency.

The nurturing and education of children is an exercise in soulcraft. The organization and administration of schools is a spiritual endeavor. The Court's intrusion into school policy represented no small enlargement of its cultural magisterium, already formidable by virtue of its authority over celebrations and persecutions.

It is time to ask: Is there something in the Constitution of the United States that invites the Court, the legal profession, and finally the nation, to follow this path? Something that pushes toward a reading of the First Amendment in which neither Congress, nor any state legislature, may make religious law — while the Supreme Court not only may, but is expected to do so?

Chapter Four: A Secular Scripture

Preamble

We the people of the United States, in order to form a more perfect Union, establish Justice, insure domestic Tranquility, provide for the common defence, promote the general Welfare, and secure the Blessings of Liberty to ourselves and our Posterity, do ordain and establish this Constitution for the United States of America.

What point might there be in speaking of the Constitution as a scripture?

Both the Bible and the Constitution offer guidance as to profound questions and perennial conflicts. The Bible becomes explicitly legal in some passages, especially in the Decalogue. On the other hand, the American Declaration of Independence opened with a religious vision, a vision quickly coupled with a list of very earthy and specific grievances against the King of England. And the Constitution, eleven years later, sought to make the Declaration's vision a reality.

When we say "Thou shalt!" or "Thou shalt not!" our motives may be several. Probably our motives are usually several, not singular; nor must any particular motive be either sacred or mundane, either religious or secular. The law, as shown in the cases previously discussed, often enough cannot avoid touching upon sacred concerns.

But there are arguments, of course, against according the Constitution scriptural status.

For one: Already, in the Preamble, our expectations for the new government are turned away from the idea of transcendence, away from any expectation of deliverance from human limits and vulnerabilities and sufferings. It appears there that the statesmen of Philadelphia were not trying to map the very narrowest and steepest paths along which so many saintly souls have toiled over the ages. Salvation, if on their minds at all, might seem to have been set to one side, or left in the background. "Render unto Caesar the things that are Caesar's, and unto God the things that are God's." The distinction is ancient; and the constitutional authors focused a great deal of their attention upon the challenge of rendering appropriately unto Caesar.

Still, if this idea, the City of Man versus the City of God, provides a frame of mind and a basic direction for the Constitution, we need to keep in mind that it is itself a religious inheritance. It entered the world through Judaism and Christianity.

Another reservation might be found in the omission, from the purposes listed in the Preamble, of equality. Equality was the battle cry of the American Revolution. Equality was the first of the self-evident truths proclaimed in the Declaration. Equality, the Declaration had stated in so many words, is sacred. If the Declaration also, implicitly, gave the blessings of life, liberty, and the pursuit of happiness a no less exalted status, still, two of these do not appear in the Preamble. The Preamble, taken as a whole, can seem relatively mundane.

Another doubt: Surely a legal document, even so important a legal document as a constitution, ought to be predominantly mundane. Legal ambiguities may be unavoidable even in well-drafted instruments, but they are always potentially troublesome; and no concept is more intractably ambiguous than equality. Once removed from its home in the realm of mathematics, it fits at best awkwardly into the broad universe of moral and political discourse. An algorithm which can reliably distinguish beneficent equality from invidious equality, constructive equality from destructive equality, has yet to be found. None, most probably, ever will be found. The constitutional authors had good reason to treat this ideal with wariness. Two others listed in the Preamble, welfare and liberty, are also highly ambiguous; and these, along with equality, make very few appearances in the constitutional text.

* * *

What, on the other hand, might argue in favor of the title of this chapter?

"But what is government itself, but the greatest of all reflections upon human nature?" asked James Madison. He is not known to have said the same about the Bible. He would have offended many of his contemporaries had he done so. Would he have denied, however, that the Bible shines a powerful and penetrating light upon human nature? Scriptures defy neat classification. The Constitution of the United States provides an excellent study of the uncertain boundaries between political and religious life. Its authors, as they grappled with political architecture, grappled unavoidably also with spiritual ambiguity.

Consider the various purposes expressly stated in the Preamble: union, justice, domestic tranquility, the common defense, the general welfare, liberty. Any one of these blessings is no mean achievement for any people. All of them, arising together in one time and place out of the tumult and violence filling the pages of history, would seem miraculous. Their conjunction would be a kind of worldly salvation. Wouldn't the pursuit of all these earthly beatitudes, then, merit description as a sacred calling? Wouldn't a nation faithfully pursuing all of them need to become a kingdom of priests? Wouldn't such a nation look for something resembling sainthood in its leaders?

Furthermore, proceeding through the constitutional text, the careful reader will realize that it represents, unevenly but recurrently, an essay upon the principles and practices of civic equality. And civic equality, although a narrower concept than equality in full (whatever "equality in full" might mean), loses by the adjective little if any of the inescapable ambiguity noted above. Indeed, scholars of the Constitution debate its meaning endlessly.

Scholars of the Constitution, that is to say, treat the Constitution, often unwittingly, as if it were a scripture. The scholarly debates tend to be unproductive, however, unless they are informed by the entire constitutional text. The debates become more informative if they are shaped as well by the history that followed upon the ratification of the Constitution in 1789. Many argue that the statesmen of Philadelphia have proven themselves, over the course of two centuries and more, honest and thoughtful, if cautious, egalitarians. Perhaps an honest and thoughtful egalitarian must be a cautious egalitarian. Certainly the constitutional authors handled the ideal discreetly and carefully within the four corners of the document they created.

The Constitution is surely more than just a reflection upon equality and a prescription for equality. But it definitely has that character. Few of its earliest readers would have quarreled with the description; for hierarchies and aristocracies of many kinds were pervasive, in thought and in deed, throughout their world. The Constitution of the United States renewed the quest for democracy which had animated, briefly, the Athenian city-state and the Roman Republic; but renewed it in a more sophisticated way. In a document representing the combined wisdom of several dozen thoughtful admirers of the ancient republics, the American founders laid out a very new plan for a very old political endeavor. To call that document a scripture seems appropriate enough.

What follows are reflections upon the constitutional text in light of these questions and concerns. Passages of the Constitution subsequently changed or deleted are placed between brackets and italicized.

Article I.

Section 1. All legislative Powers herein granted shall be vested in a Congress of the United States, which shall consist of a Senate and House of Representatives.

Section 2. The House of Representatives shall be composed of Members chosen every second Year by the People of the several States, and the Electors in each State shall have the Qualifications requisite for Electors of the most numerous Branch of the State Legislature.

No Person shall be a Representative who shall not have attained to the Age of twenty five Years, and been seven Years a Citizen of the United States, and who shall not, when elected, be an Inhabitant of that State in which he shall be chosen.

[*Representatives and direct Taxes shall be apportioned among the several States which may be included within this Union, according to the respective Numbers, which shall be determined by adding to the whole Number of free Persons, including those bound to Service for a Term of Years, and excluding Indians not taxed, three fifths of all other Persons.*] The actual Enumeration shall be made within three Years after the first Meeting of the Congress of the United States, and within every subsequent Term of ten Years, in such Manner as they shall by Law direct. The number of Representatives shall not exceed one for every thirty Thousand, but each State shall have at Least one Representative; and until such enumeration shall be made, the State of New Hampshire shall be entitled to chuse three, Massachusetts eight, Rhode-Island and Providence Plantations one, Connecticut five, New-York six, New Jersey four, Pennsylvania eight, Delaware one, Maryland six, Virginia ten, North Carolina five, South Carolina five, and Georgia three.

When vacancies happen in the Representation from any State, the Executive Authority thereof shall issue writs of Election to fill such Vacancies.

The House of Representatives shall chuse their Speaker and other Officers; and shall have the sole Power of Impeachment.

Section 3. The Senate of the United States shall be composed of two Senators from each State, [*chosen by the Legislature thereof,*] for six Years; and each Senator shall have one Vote.

Immediately after they shall be assembled in Consequence of the first Election, they shall be divided as equally as may be into three Classes. The Seats of the Senators of the first Class shall be vacated at the Expiration of the second Year, of the second Class at the Expiration of the fourth Year, and of the third Class at the Expiration of the sixth Year, so that one third may be chosen every second Year; [*and if Vacancies happen by Resignation, or otherwise, during the Recess of the Legislature of any State, the Executive thereof may make temporary Appointments until the next Meeting of the Legislature, which shall then fill such Vacancies.*]

No Person shall be a Senator who shall not have attained to the Age of thirty Years, and been nine Years a Citizen of the United States, and who shall not, when elected, be an Inhabitant of that State for which he shall be chosen.

The Vice President of the United States shall be President of the Senate, but shall have no Vote, unless they be equally divided.

The Senate shall chuse their other Officers, and also a President pro tempore, in the Absence of the Vice President, or when he shall exercise the Office of President of the United States.

The Senate shall have the sole Power to try all Impeachments. When sitting for that Purpose, they shall be on Oath or Affirmation. When the President of the United States is tried, the Chief Justice shall preside: And no Person shall be convicted without the Concurrence of two thirds of the Members present.

Judgment in Cases of Impeachment shall not extend further than to removal from Office, and disqualification to hold and enjoy any Office of honor, Trust or Profit under the United States: but the Party convicted shall nevertheless be liable and subject to Indictment, Trial, Judgment and Punishment, according to Law.

Section 4. The Times, Places and Manner of holding Elections for Senators and Representatives, shall be prescribed in each State by the Legislature thereof; but the Congress may at any time by Law make or alter such Regulations, except as to the Places of chusing Senators.

The Congress shall assemble at least once in every Year, and such Meeting shall be [*on the first Monday in December,*] unless they shall by Law appoint a different Day.

Section 5. Each House shall be the Judge of the Elections, Returns and Qualifications of its own Members, and a Majority of each shall constitute a Quorum to do Business; but a smaller Number may adjourn from day to day, and may be authorized to compel the Attendance of absent Members, in such Manner, and under such Penalties as each House may provide.

Each House may determine the Rules of its Proceedings, punish its Members for disorderly Behaviour, and, with the Concurrence of two thirds, expel a Member.

Each House shall keep a Journal of its Proceedings, and from time to time publish the same, excepting such Parts as may in their Judgment require Secrecy; and the Yeas and Nays of the Members of either House on any question shall, at the Desire of one fifth of those Present, be entered on the Journal.

Neither House, during the Session of Congress, shall, without the Consent of the other, adjourn for more than three days, nor to any other Place than that in which the two Houses shall be sitting.

Section 6. The Senators and Representatives shall receive a Compensation for their Services, to be ascertained by Law, and paid out of the Treasury of the United States. They shall in all Cases, except Treason, Felony, and Breach of the Peace, be privileged from Arrest during their Attendance at the Session of their respective Houses, and in going to and returning from the same; and for any Speech or Debate in either House, they shall not be questioned in any other Place.

No Senator or Representative shall, during the Time for which he was elected, be appointed to any civil Office under the authority of the United States, which shall have been created, or the emoluments whereof shall have been encreased during such time; and no Person holding any Office under the United States, shall be a Member of either House during his Continuance in Office.

Section 7. All bills for raising Revenue shall originate in the House of Representatives; but the Senate may propose or concur with Amendments as on other Bills.

Every Bill which shall have passed the House of Representatives and the Senate, shall, before it becomes a Law, be presented to the President of the United

States; If he approve he shall sign it, but if not he shall return it, with his Objections to that House in which it shall have originated, who shall enter the Objections at large on their Journal, and proceed to reconsider it. If after such Reconsideration two thirds of that House shall agree to pass the Bill, it shall be sent, together with the Objections, to the other House, by which it shall likewise be reconsidered, and if approved by two thirds of that House, it shall become a Law. But in all such Cases the Votes of both Houses shall be determined by yeas and Nays, and the Names of the Persons voting for and against the Bill shall be entered on the Journal of each House respectively. If any Bill shall not be returned by the President within ten Days (Sundays excepted) after it shall have been presented to him, the Same shall be a Law, in like Manner as if he had signed it, unless the Congress by their Adjournment prevent its Return, in which case it shall not be a Law.

Every Order, Resolution, or Vote to which the Concurrence of the Senate and House of Representatives may be necessary (except on a question of Adjournment) shall be presented to the President of the United States; and before the Same shall take Effect, shall be approved by him, or being disapproved by him, shall be repassed by two thirds of the Senate and House of Representatives, according to the Rules and Limitations prescribed in the Cases of a Bill.

Section 8. The Congress shall have Power to lay and collect Taxes, Duties, Imposts and Excises, to pay the Debts and provide for the common Defense and general Welfare of the United States; but all Duties, Imposts and Excises shall be uniform throughout the United States;

To borrow Money on the credit of the United States;

To regulate Commerce with foreign Nations, and among the several States, and with the Indian tribes;

To establish an uniform Rule of Naturalization, and uniform Laws on the subject of Bankruptcies throughout the United States;

To coin Money, regulate the Value thereof, and of foreign Coin, and fix the standard of weights and Measures;

To provide for the Punishment of counterfeiting the Securities and current Coin of the United States;

To establish Post Offices and post Roads;

To promote the Progress of Science and useful Arts, by securing for limited Times to Authors and Inventors the exclusive Right to their respective Writings and Discoveries;

To constitute tribunals inferior to the supreme Court;

To define and punish Piracies and felonies committed on the high Seas, and Offenses against the Law of Nations;

To declare War, grant Letters of Marque and Reprisal, and make Rules concerning Captures on Land and Water;

To raise and support Armies, but no Appropriation of Money to that Use shall be for a longer Term than two Years;

To provide and maintain a Navy;

To make Rules for the Government and Regulation of the land and naval Forces;

To provide for calling forth the Militia to execute the Laws of the Union, suppress Insurrections and repel Invasions;

To provide for organizing, arming, and disciplining, the Militia, and for governing such Part of them as may be employed in the Service of the United States, reserving to the States respectively , the Appointment of the Officers, and the Authority of training the Militia according to the discipline prescribed by Congress;

To exercise exclusive Legislation in all Cases whatsoever, over such District (not exceeding ten Miles square) as may, by Cession of particular States, and the Acceptance of Congress, become the Seat of the Government of the United States, and to exercise like Authority over all Places purchased by the Consent of the Legislature of the State in which the Same shall be, for the Erection of Forts, Magazines, Arsenals, dock-Yards and other needful Buildings; — And

To make all Laws which shall be necessary and proper for carrying into Execution the foregoing Powers, and other Powers vested by this Constitution in the Government of the United States, or in any Department or Officer thereof.

Section 9. The Migration or Importation of such Persons as any of the States now existing shall think proper to admit, shall not be prohibited by the Congress prior to the Year one thousand eight hundred and eight, but a Tax or duty may be imposed on such Importation, not exceeding ten dollars for each Person.

The Privilege of the Writ of Habeas Corpus shall not be suspended, unless when in Cases of Rebellion or Invasion the Public Safety may require it.

No Bill of Attainder or ex post facto Law shall be passed.

No Capitation, or other direct, Tax shall be laid, unless in Proportion to the Census or Enumeration herein before directed to be taken.

No Tax or Duty shall be laid on Articles exported from any State.

No Preference shall be given by any Regulation of Commerce or Revenue to the Ports of one State over those of another; nor shall Vessels bound to, or from, one State, be obliged to enter, clear, or pay Duties in another.

No Money shall be drawn from the Treasury, but in Consequence of Appropriations made by Law; and a regular Statement and Account of the Receipts and Expenditures of all public Money shall be published from time to time.

No Title of Nobility shall be granted by the United States: And no Person holding any Office of Profit or Trust under them, shall, without the Consent of the Congress, accept of any present, Emolument, Office, or Title, of any kind whatever, from any King, Prince, or foreign State.

Section 10. No State shall enter into any Treaty, Alliance, or Confederation; grant Letters of Marque and Reprisal; coin Money; emit Bills of Credit; make any Thing but gold and silver coin a Tender in Payment of Debts; pass any Bill of Attainder, ex post facto Law, or Law impairing the Obligation of Contracts, or grant any Title of Nobility.

> No State shall, without the Consent of the Congress, lay any Imposts or Duties on Imports or Exports, except what may be absolutely necessary for executing its inspection Laws; and the Net Produce of all Duties and Imposts, laid by any State on Imports or Exports, shall be for the Use of the Treasury of the United States; and all such Laws shall be subject to the Revision and Controul of the Congress.
>
> No State shall, without the Consent of Congress, lay any Duty of Tonnage, keep Troops, or Ships of War in time of Peace, enter into any Agreement or Compact with another State, or with a foreign Power, or engage in War, unless actually invaded, or in such imminent Danger as will not admit of delay.

In Section 1 of Article I, the constitutional authors laid their first offering upon the altar of equality: a foundation of law. Good legislators strive to treat like cases alike. They are sensitive to the charge of official capriciousness. They try to avoid random, or unprincipled, or self-interested uses of power. They seek a rule or standard which is intelligible and general. A government which governs through genuine legislation, rather than by fiat or edict, is already, to that extent, egalitarian.

Even so, the egalitarianism of a system of law may be very limited. One of the Roman emperors oversaw the creation of a workable and sensible, and long-used, legal code. More is needed. And immediately after Article I Section 1 came the second offering. Sections 2 and 3 made the nation's legislators answerable to the electorates which sent them to Congress. They were to gain their authority, directly or indirectly, from the citizens of one or another of the many local American communities. They were to retain that authority, or lose it, through periodic elections. They were made quite sensitive to the beliefs and interests of their constituents.

In these two fundamental ways, American legislators were encouraged to treat their constituents as civic equals.

Much remained to be specified, of course. Critics are quick to highlight various historical limitations upon the franchise. But two essential components of an egalitarian social order were firmly planted in the opening sections of the Constitution.

* * *

Then, proceeding further into Article I, we encounter in Section 8 a remarkable novelty — a real bifurcation of government, an extensive division of power between the local governments and the new central government. Article I Section 8 confirmed the limited character of the new government, a character already suggested by the Preamble. This lengthy provision listed the legitimate functions of the central authority. To grasp the significance of what we read there, however, we must read negatively as well as positively. We must pay careful attention to what is missing from the list in Section 8. Pondering the powers entrusted to Congress, we must ponder at the same time the many powers quite deliberately not entrusted to Congress. Thus:

> Nothing appears in Section 8 about the establishment of a national church, or about the conduct of religious life more generally.

> Nothing is found there about the regulation of speech or the press; nor about the law of defamation and obscenity.

> Nothing about the relations between men and women; nor about the laws of marriage, or family relations, or inheritance.

> Nothing about the definition or regulation of property.

> Nothing about the policing or the punishment of crime.

> Nothing about the law of contracts.

> Nothing about the redress of injuries, sometimes referred to as the law of torts.

Nothing about the professions of law, or medicine, or banking.

Nothing about the education of new generations.

Nothing about literature and the other arts, except the securing to authors and inventors the fruits of their creations.

Nothing about charity, nothing about public responsibilities toward the poor and the disadvantaged.

Even as to the regulation of commerce, an unavoidable responsibility of governments, Congressional authority was limited to trade across state lines and beyond the nation's boundaries.

Section 8 left to the local authorities what it did not expressly commit to Congress. Numerous foundational elements of a social order, numerous formative influences upon the character and conduct of a people, were to remain local responsibilities. Officials of the nation were assigned other concerns and other duties.

* * *

But what, it is fair to ask, could Section 8, with its extensive partitioning of American government, have to do with civic equality?

The question might puzzle a good many Americans today. It would have puzzled few in the late eighteenth century. Most citizens of the Colonies and the early Republic seldom traveled far from home. Those who did often encountered not only different sights and sounds, but different ways of life. Americans of that earlier time, venturing across a political boundary, could find themselves amidst an almost alien culture. When this happened, they would have learned more about their own culture. Many might well have come to appreciate, perhaps even to cherish their own culture. Many might have been moved to defend their own culture — and to grant other Americans, living in distant communities, a right to cherish and defend theirs.

Cultural pluralism's social and political effects were doubt-less mixed and sometimes ambiguous. But one of those effects, surely, was the teaching of civic equality.

We should hardly be surprised, then, to find the constitu-tional authors leaving to local governments a thick portfolio of concerns and authorities. The ratification of the Constitution left those numerous governments in place as vigorous sovereignties. The states remained in the best position to focus aspirations; to channel energies; to celebrate some pursuits and passions, and to discourage others. The local governments were the curators and custodians of civic culture in the early Republic. To a large extent the citizens of different states were both political and cultural equals. Article I Section 8 made the states the building blocks of a nation compounded from diverse regions and cities.

To put this a little differently: American equality, the civic equality contemplated by the Constitution, was intended to encompass groups and communities, no less than individuals. It is arguable that American equality focused more upon groups and associations, than upon individuals. Local communities in the early American Republic had a panoply of rights, as communities.

Our political forebears called this states' rights. As a social phenomenon both political and cultural, however, we can better call it localism, or pluralism. One good illustration of it can be drawn by contrast. The Jacobins, who were busily upending the old regime in France in 1791, showed suspicion and even hostility towards associations of citizens independent of the national government.[13] Here is a historical curiosity. French and American patriots were both ardently pursuing civic equality at about the same time, but in quite different ways.

Today, with two centuries and more of political experience, we can see more clearly the problems which were inherent in the regional and cultural equalities of the early Republic. Perhaps we can see more clearly also the promise, and the virtues, of this

---

[13] See the law named after Le Chapelier, passed June 14, 1791.

most innovative statecraft. But that is a task for historians and political philosophers. Here we are examining the constitutional text. Here we need to note that numerous local communities were expected not only to cooperate with one another, but were enabled also to contend with one another on a footing of relative political and cultural equality.

Here, that is, we need to recognize and highlight the very extensive pluralism which was a third fundamental feature of the American Republic. We need to add that feature to the first two: the legal order, and governmental accountability to the governed.

Nor, under the heading of pluralism, is it out of place here to anticipate the co-equality of the three distinct branches of the new central government — the denial of supreme authority to any one of them — which will follow in the next two Articles. The idea of divided sovereignty was not new in 1787. The pattern was already in place in the state governments. The idea is that the existence of multiple centers of political power, each having its own revenues and its own particular functions, tends to limit the ambitions and moderate the actions of prominent officials; to impede the formation of narrow but powerful coalitions of interest and purpose; and thus to prevent an excessive concentration of power in any single sect or faction.

The division of sovereign power, in other words, is itself an egalitarian political measure.

Article II

Section 1. The executive Power shall be vested in a President of the United States of America. He shall hold his Office during the Term of four Years, and, together with the Vice President, chosen for the same Term, be elected, as follows.

Each State shall appoint, in such Manner as the Legislature thereof may direct, a Number of Electors, equal to the whole Number of Senators and Representatives to which the State may be entitled in the Congress:

but no Senator or Representative, or Person holding an Office of Trust or Profit under the United States, shall be appointed an Elector.

[*The Electors shall meet in their respective states, and vote by Ballot for two Persons, of whom one at least shall not be an Inhabitant of the same State with themselves. And they shall make a List of all the Persons voted for, and of the Number of Votes for each; which List they shall sign and certify, and transmit sealed to the Seat of the Government of the United States, directed to the President of the Senate. The President of the Senate shall, in the Presence of the Senate and House of Representatives, open all the Certificates, and the Votes shall then be counted. The Person having the greatest Number of Votes shall be the President, if such Number be a Majority of the whole Number of Electors appointed; and if there be more than one who have such majority, and have an equal number of Votes, then the House of Representatives, shall immediately chuse by Ballot one of them for President; and if no Person have a Majority, then from the five highest on the List the said House shall in like Manner chuse the President. But in chusing the President, the Votes shall be taken by States, the Representation from each State having one Vote; A quorum for this Purpose shall consist of a Member or Members from two thirds of the States, and a majority of all the States shall be necessary to a Choice. In every Case, after the Choice of the President, the Person having the greatest Number of Votes of the Electors shall be the Vice President. But if there should remain two or more who have equal Votes, the Senate shall chuse from them by Ballot the Vice President.*]

The Congress may determine the Time of chusing he Electors, and the day on which they shall give their Votes; which Day shall be the same throughout the United States.

No Person except a natural born Citizen, or a Citizen of the United States, at the time of the Adoption of this Constitution, shall be eligible to the Office of

President; neither shall any person be eligible to that Office who shall not have attained to the Age of thirty five Years, and been fourteen Years a Resident within the United States.

[In Case of the Removal of the President from Office, or of his Death, Resignation, or Inability to discharge the Powers and Duties of the said Office, the Same shall devolve on the Vice President, and the Congress may by Law provide for the Case of Removal, Death, Resignation or Inability, both of the President and Vice President, declaring what Officer shall the act as President, and such Officer shall act accordingly, until the Disability be removed, or a President shall be elected.]

The President shall, at stated Times, receive for his Services, a Compensation, which shall neither be increased nor diminished during the Period for which he shall have been elected, and he shall not receive within that Period any other Emolument from the United States, or any of them.

Before he enter on the Execution of his Office, he shall take the following Oath or Affirmation: — "I do solemnly swear (or affirm) that I will faithfully execute the Office of President of the United States, and will to the best of my Ability, preserve, protect and defend the Constitution of the United States."

Section 2. The President shall be Commander in Chief of the Army and Navy of the United States, and of the Militia of the several States, when called into the actual Service of the United States; he may require the Opinion, in writing, of the principal Officer in each of the executive Departments, upon any Subject relating to the Duties of their respective Offices, and he shall have Power to grant Reprieves and Pardons for Offenses against the United States, except in cases of Impeachment.

He shall have Power, by and with the Advice and Consent of the Senate, to make Treaties, provided two thirds of the Senators present concur; and he shall nominate, and by and with the Advice and Consent of the Senate, shall appoint Ambassadors, other public Ministers and Consuls, Judges of the Supreme court, and all other Officers of the United States, whose Appointments are not herein otherwise provided for, and which shall be established by Law: but the Congress may by Law vest the Appointment of such inferior Officers, as they think Proper, in the President Alone, in the Courts of Law, or in the Heads of Departments.

The President shall have Power to fill up all Vacancies that may happen during the Recess of the Senate, by granting Commissions which shall expire at the End of their next Session.

Section 3. He shall from time to time give to the Congress Information of the State of the Union, and recommend to their Consideration such Measures as he shall judge necessary and expedient; he may, on extraordinary Occasions, convene both Houses, or either of them, and in Case of Disagreement between them, with Respect to the Time of Adjournment, he may adjourn them to such Time as he shall think proper; he shall receive Ambassadors and other public Ministers; he shall take Care that the Laws be faithfully executed, and shall Commission all the Officers of the United States.

Section 4. The President, Vice President and all civil Officers of the United States, shall be removed from Office on Impeachment for, and Conviction of, Treason, Bribery, or other high Crimes and Misdemeanors.

In Article II we find the constitutional authors balancing their egalitarian convictions against other concerns. Recognizing that extraordinary problems and dangers may require prompt and decisive leadership, they vested in the American President a number of powers. They gave this singular official the ability to act effectively in behalf of the entire nation when necessary. They sought to calibrate the inevitable tension between the republican ideal of civic equality, and the perennial necessity of authority, or hierarchy. They sought to provide a political inequality adequate to the nation's needs, without fatally compromising its republican character.

In Article II, we might say, they injected an antigen into the egalitarian body politic, hoping to invigorate it while leaving its fundamentally democratic system healthy. Clearly they recognized the risks involved in creating so formidable a public officer. Their wariness can be seen in the countermeasures they took against Presidential ambition and willfulness.

One safeguard: the term of office, four years, after which its occupant must seek reelection.

Another: the complications involved in filling the office. The President was to be chosen by a considerable number of subordinate elected officials drawn from every state in the Union. A similar method of decision was provided for an election lacking a clear winner, and for replacement of a disabled President. The purpose of these rather elaborate measures seems to have been a refinement of the popular will, testing it against the judgment of numerous experienced leaders. The authors may have felt also that these procedures would favor candidates whose appeal was felt across the nation, not just in the larger cities and states.

Another precaution: The President's domestic functions are to enforce the laws, and to appoint, subject to legislative approval, judges and subordinate executive officials. His need to ground these actions in the will of the nation's citizenry tends to make the President, when the constitutional arrangements work properly, a leader attentive to and solicitous of the many.

Nor must we overlook the power of the national legisla-tors to impeach and remove a President who commits "treason, bribery, or other high crimes and misdemeanors."

These four hedges against Presidential power exemplify one or the other of the first two egalitarian principles already embedded in Article I: the legal order, and the accountability of officials to citizens. But the other salient feature of Article I, the bifurcation of American government, should not be overlooked here. For the authority of the agencies which the President controls, after all, was to extend to only a part of the nation's governance — and not, in general, a large part. The federal system itself, with its heavy emphasis upon the local and the regional, tended to curtail the reach and scope of the national executive.

A zealous egalitarian may belittle these checks upon the President. He may regard them as flimsy if not useless against an adroit and determined chief executive. His concerns may be well placed. But the challenge of articulating a dependably safe way to provide focused and vigorous republican leadership presents no small difficulty. Few will be convinced, moreover, that the need for such leadership can be safely ignored.

* * *

Are we to conclude that Article II contributes nothing further to the elucidation of American equality?

The perspective has definitely shifted. With Article II we begin looking at measures directed against the dangers of too much equality: against too many discordant and potent factions, against too much dissension in the public councils, against delay and indecisiveness in dangerous circumstances. Tensions in the new government come to the fore here. Yet we can hardly speak of paradox, for tensions are inevitable in any form of govern-ment. Indeed, within limits, open public tensions may well be signs of political good health.

Perhaps, then, our understanding of equality is enlarged by Article II. Perhaps, in an important sense, the executive office itself represents a thesis about equality — in this case, a thesis about the limitations of equality. For the President is political authority incarnate, as fully incarnate as the constitutional authors considered likely to be compatible with republican government.

In Article II, then, we have a critique, limited but important, of egalitarian enthusiasms. Perfect equality, comprehensive equality, implied the statesmen of Philadelphia, is a chimera. No stable and just and enduring social order can meet such a standard. There must be inequalities, sometimes quite sharp inequalities, even where civic equality generally prevails. Vigorous and responsible government will sometimes necessitate a neglect of the preferences and judgments of many citizens; sometimes, perhaps, even the overriding of those preferences and judgments.

In Article II we can discern a fourth principle of American equality, another hypothesis about equality. The dangers of too determined a pursuit of equality, or a naïve understanding of equality, come to the fore.

Article III

Section 1. The judicial Power of the United States, shall be vested in one supreme Court, and in such inferior Courts as the Congress may from time to time ordain and establish. The Judges, both of the supreme and inferior Courts, shall hold their Offices during good Behaviour, and shall, at stated Times, receive for their Services, a Compensation, which shall not be diminished during their Continuance in Office.

Section 2. The judicial Power shall extend to all Cases, in Law and Equity, arising under this Constitution, the Laws of the United States, and Treaties made, or which shall be made, under their Authority; — to all Cases affecting Ambassadors, other public Ministers and Consuls; — to all Cases of admiralty and maritime Jurisdiction; — to Controversies to which the United States shall be a Party; — to Controversies between two or more States; — [between a State and Citizens of *another State; –]* between Citizens of different States; — between Citizens of the same State claiming Lands under Grants of different States, [*and between a State, or the Citizens thereof, and foreign States, Citizens or Subjects.*]

In all Cases affecting Ambassadors, other public Ministers and Consuls, and those in which a State shall be Party, the supreme Court shall have original Jurisdiction. In all the other Cases before mentioned, the supreme Court shall have appellate Jurisdiction, both as to Law and Fact, with such exceptions, and under such Regulations as the Congress shall make.

The Trial of all Crimes, except in Cases of Impeachment; shall be by Jury; and such Trial shall be held in the State where the said Crimes shall have been committed; but when not committed within any State, the Trial shall be at such Place or Places as the Congress may by Law have directed.

Section 3. Treason against the United States, shall consist only in levying War against them, or in adhering to their Enemies, giving them Aid and Comfort. No Person shall be convicted of Treason unless on the Testimony of two Witnesses to the same overt Act, or on Confession in open Court.

The Congress shall have Power to declare the Punishment of Treason, but no Attainder of Treason shall work Corruption of Blood, or Forfeiture except during the Life of the Person attainted.

The statesmen of 1787 tried to separate the nation's judges from political distractions and partisan animosities. Each was given tenure for life and guaranteed a fixed compensation. Each was made free of any routine accountability to either voters or elected officials. Each was put in a position to perform the important judicial responsibilities effectively, independently, and impartially. Equality gave way to hierarchy, as it had in Article II. The American judiciary forms a second line of defense against the perils of a too comprehensive equality.

But then that judiciary itself poses risks to the constitutional project. The compatibility of the judges with republican government is not immediately obvious. Seated upon the bench, robed, gavel in hand, they look like aristocrats or oligarchs. These few officials comprise a small and powerful elite among the American political classes. They are potentates within their courtrooms, and they are not to be trifled with wherever their writ may run. Sensible persons do not want their conduct or their affairs under scrutiny by one of the nation's judges; for at best, such dealings tend to be complex and expensive.

What, then, would remind the judges, and incline them, to remain respectful and responsive toward their fellow citizens? How did the constitutional authors expect to keep zealots and eccentrics and empire-builders off the judicial bench? How did they hope to prevent abuse of the judicial power?

* * *

We encountered in Article I three political arrangements, three institutions built into the Constitution to promote equality among citizens of the United States. Of those three, two were employed as a counterbalance to the foreseeable temptations attending judicial office.

Most fundamentally: devoted service to the legal order was to be the judge's special calling and discipline. His responsibility was to apply the nation's laws to specific cases brought before him by litigants in conflict. Judges were not to go in search of controversies. They were not to become political entrepreneurs. They were to serve as quasi-technicians, we might say, keeping the legal principle — like cases to be treated alike — in good working order. They were not to become legislators.

The judicial approach to controversy, moreover, was expected to bear a certain character. Judges were not to speculate. Visions and prophecies were to be no part of their business. The arguments supporting a judge's decision, besides being focused upon the circumstances of the dispute before him, were to be carefully informed by the laws, the customs, and the way of life of the American people. These judicial proprieties were inherited from the mother country, Britain, in which an impressive legal tradition had evolved over hundreds of years.

American judges would be called upon, of course, to interpret statutes enacted by legislators. They would find themselves adapting older judicial rulings or doctrines to new situations. They would begin, early on, to assess the adherence of other authorities, national and local, to constitutional principles. These can be fine lines to walk. There are ambiguous cases. But clearly the nation's judges were given no general commission to innovate, or to revise the laws to accord with their sense of the zeitgeist.

* * *

In addition to the ideals of the legal order, the constitutional authors made use of the principle of accountability. That principle underlay the forms and procedures of judicial appointment, which tended to put equable and prudent new judges on the bench. No citizen of markedly domineering temperament or alarming views was likely to be chosen by the President and approved by the Senate.

Further, once a new judge took office, there was the liability of all national officials, elective and appointive, to impeachment and removal; although the standard of propriety set for judges, their good behavior, seemed to emphasize personal conduct rather than official actions.

The principle of accountability was implicit also in the authority given Congress to delete from the jurisdiction of the nation's courts those topics considered unsuitable for judicial resolution. With a sufficient consensus among them that the judiciary was overreaching, Senators and Representatives could reserve to themselves selected policies and controversies. This legislative power should give a thoughtful judge pause before he issues a politically-charged ruling.

The reader will note, however, that the third of the egalitarian arrangements found in Article I, the principle of pluralism, is missing here. The idea of diversity or collegiality makes no formal appearance in Article III. The nation's judiciary is unified. It is a hierarchy, with the Supreme Court at its apex. There seems to have been a general assumption that the highest court would consist of several judges, a majority of whom would issue rulings. But those rulings would be final. The Court would interpret the law for all citizens of the United States.

The definition of the judicial office, the manner in which the judiciary is staffed, plus the limited powers of oversight given the Congress, may tend to make judges good and faithful officials of the American Republic. But that is the most we can say.

* * *

With the completion of Articles I, II, and III, the constitutional authors had put in place the basic structures and operations of the central government of the United States. In Article I, seeking to ensure that the new government would answer to the governed, and serve the governed, they prescribed three general patterns of political interaction: the legal order; electoral accountability; and a pluralism both political and cultural. With these, they sought to create and sustain a substantial and effective civic equality. In Articles II and III they tempered or checked that equality with carefully designed countermeasures of inequality. They built limited hierarchies for specific purposes.

Necessarily they were doing more. In designing republican institutions they were implicitly delineating a social type, an ideal character, whom they thought capable of self-government. They knew that the republic they envisioned required citizens appreciative of its liberties and equal to its demands. In laying the foundations for a broad-based politics of respect and discussion and cooperation, the statesmen of 1787 were also painting a portrait of the republican persona.

Let us shift the perspective, then. Let us turn from the question of institutional form to that of personal character. As to the political forms and methods outlined in Articles I, II, and III, let us ask: What kind of habits, or expectations, or virtues, are posited there?

* * *

For one: A well-administered legal order teaches its citizens how to question themselves. As they invoke a particular law in their own behalf, or as they sit on a jury, they are prompted to ask: Would I accept this law's claim upon me? Am I prepared to follow the rules, and meet the standards, which I expect of others?

This requires a mature measure of self-awareness. Surely that is important for citizens of a republic, if they are to consider themselves and their neighbors as like cases, as legal equals. The golden rule, or its silver variant — do not do unto others as you would not have them do unto you — must inform the ethos of such a people.

The good republican citizen, let us say, needs a lively sense of reciprocity toward others.

* * *

For another: The regular electoral accountability of officials to voters generates a lot of public activity. There are ongoing contacts and discussions among the many who are concerned. Associations come into being, a great variety of them, keeping their members focused upon a wide range of different situations and interests. Ideally, before a law is enacted or amended, or a new policy adopted, the preferences and judgments of a representative sample of citizens are consulted. Ideally, those preferences and judgments are accommodated to the extent that they can be. Ideally, due respect is accorded all participants, even though some, perhaps many, will inevitably be displeased with the outcome.

All of this, too, teaches reciprocity. But it teaches more. Beyond that essential sentiment, habits of no less importance are widely cultivated. Many learn to pay attention to public affairs. Many go further, finding a voice and becoming participants. These habits, let us say, produce a corps of political activists.

Still, that activity, in a republic, needs to be of a certain character. Republican activists, even as they contend against one another, at the same time are able to tend and maintain the sense of equality which is the foundation of a republic. They will be partisans in one sense. The best of them, however, will be more than that. They will be colleagues, perhaps even friends, in serving their fellow citizens.

* * *

What about localism, or pluralism? What character traits are nourished among numerous smaller communities which make their own laws and manage their own affairs?

Here very pragmatic considerations come into play. One is geography. In a nation of continental extent, local cultures may vary widely. Different topographies, different economies, different histories resist standardization. Pressures toward uniformity provoke resentment and resistance.

Numbers become important also. The government of a vast populace will necessarily be directed by a very few. The lines of communication will all too easily become clogged and tangled. There are too many interests to be considered, too many perspectives, too much divergence of opinion, too little time and energy for careful deliberation. Most people, under these circumstances, finding too much difficulty making themselves heard, will withdraw into narrower circles. Opportunities will multiply for confusion, for corruption, for deceit. It is a great error to ignore the scale upon which political interactions take place — or fail to take place. It is to ignore a central determinant of civic manners and methods. Citizens of neighboring munici-palities may consider one another's different laws and prac-tices unappealing. They may overlook those laws and practices and get along well enough, however — if they are not pushed toward one way or the other way, if conformity is not pressed upon them. But pressures toward conformity are the stock in trade of large and highly centralized organizations.

Thus it is that good republicans flourish amidst associa-tions which are many and various. Families, churches, busi-ness organizations, city councils, and regional legislatures are their training grounds and their most comfortable habitat. In these, their natural settings, they learn to accommodate others without sacrificing anyone's dignity or integrity. They learn the virtue of tolerance.

* * *

That the forms of civic equality just described might bring forth citizens who offer and expect reciprocity; who pay attention and participate; and who are tolerant toward others — none of this seems surprising. Yet Articles II and III introduce some very sharp civic inequalities. Is this a paradox? What character traits do those especially powerful officers, Presidents and judges, contribute to republican government?

The constitutional authors did their work on the basis of an assumption about political life — indeed, about social life in general. They assumed that hierarchy is intrinsic to the human condition; that among large numbers, amidst persons of all ages, inclinations, talents, training, and circumstances, leadership is necessary, that leaders must inevitably emerge.

Let us assume that the constitutional authors were correct. And let us note the corollary: that obedience, of one form or another, upon one occasion or another, to one degree or another; obedience to persons and to traditions, is the common lot, the fate of most people, most of the time.

Wouldn't a clear-eyed look around us confirm both the assumption and the corollary? Childhood — our long dependence upon parents and teachers, our need for guidance as we learn a complex way of life — offers the most obvious evidence. But as adults also we live among many and various kinds of hierarchies, we are called upon to render many and various kinds of deference and obedience. The lives and fates of those few who escape this pervasive condition often suggest that their privilege is at best a mixed blessing.

The Constitution of the United States cultivates a great virtue in the soil of stern necessity. It tries to coax thoughtful and willing obedience out of rote obedience, or compelled obedience. The constitutional forms and procedures aim at the conversion of power into authority. Mere power forces obedience. Genuine authority earns obedience. Legitimate authority can elicit enthusiastic and creative obedience.

There are several ways in which this can occur.

Elections are rich with the symbolism of reciprocity and accountability. They are ceremonies of initiation, in which aspirants to office test their merit and earn support. A would-be legislator begins as an obedient citizen; acquires a measure of power and prominence if successful; and becomes subject to authority again upon retiring or losing an election. So it is with the President and his appointees. Judges, too, will have been citizens first; most will become citizens again by retiring from the judicial office. The ongoing rotation — obedience earning authority, authority giving way to obedience — reminds all, again and again, that they are citizens among citizens.

Power becomes authority in other ways and other settings. The leader of a thriving private organization personifies skill and dependability and foresight. He gathers supporters and recruits subordinates by inspiring confidence. And when he neglects to earn his power, if he forgets that he needs to earn his power, he may well lose it.

An effective military leader is one who has faced the dangers of armed conflict with courage and resourcefulness. His demonstrated skill and valor earn him his rank and embolden the soldiers who follow him.

If hierarchies are natural, if they are unavoidable, then the concentrations of power prescribed by the Constitution are not anomalies. If hierarchies are natural and inevitable, effective republican government must accept this natural pattern and inclination, refining it and using it by anointing leaders with reciprocity and legitimacy — in a word, with authority.

Thus does a good republican citizen learn to serve others, as occasion may demand. He or she may even become a zealous servant, in causes both small and large, both private and public. Thus obedience is made compatible with dignity and civic equality. Thus thoughtful and fitting obedience takes an honored place among the republican virtues.

* * *

The sense of reciprocity; habits of active and assertive attention; a readiness to tolerate different ideas and practices, and to obey legitimate leaders: Do these four dispositions sum up the republican virtues? With these features, did the constitutional authors fill in their portrait?

Not quite. Another can be discerned within the first three Articles of the Constitution. Another schooling in civic equality is implicit there, a regimen operating most clearly in Articles I and III. The nation's legislators and judges feel the pull of a subtle but powerful egalitarian influence: the obligation of both officials and citizens to reason with one another about the law.

The questions "What should the law require?" or "What should the law prohibit?" bring into play all the legislator's experiences, all his learning, all his good will. "Come, let us reason together" summons him to transcend — not to set aside but to look beyond — his personal interests and desires, in pursuit of a wider harmony and more comprehensive justice.

In the judicial setting: The question "What is the law?" focuses attention upon the pertinent words used by the relevant legislators. It brings earlier precedents to bear upon the present. It prompts a search for context and comparison. It draws attention away from the unique circumstances, the personal emotions, the singular intuitions of the judge and the parties to a dispute.

Article III made the nation's judges especially prominent and highly visible custodians and exemplars of civic reason. Reason is the faculty called upon by those who, even as they disagree, at the same time agree — to renounce coercion. Two persons, or many, when they engage in reasoning together, tacitly recognize one another as equals. Their restrained conduct, their respectful antagonism, is a sign, a consequence, and an instrument of social and political equality. Their attentiveness towards others demonstrates their capacity for participation in a peaceful civic order.

The constitutional authors gave the nation's judges the privileges and protections they needed to make their courtrooms temples and sanctuaries of reason. In return, they asked of those judges fidelity to the legal ideal and scrupulous performance of the judicial tasks.

In this enhanced devotion to reason, in this extensive reliance upon reason, we find a fifth constitutional pillar, a fifth virtue essential to a regime of civic equality. The first instinct of a good republican citizen, faced with conflict, is to speak intelligibly, to listen well — and to argue vigorously if need be. And surely the complex system of governments outlined in 1787 required competent reasoning, and a real commitment to reasoning, not only by legislators and judges. Presidents too, and local leaders, all the way down to village aldermen, were inevitably going to encounter ambiguities as to the proper topics and limits of their authority.

* * *

One of the greatest of American Presidents, who brought the United States out of the furious passions of civil war as one nation, showed a rare genius for political and moral reasoning. And more than that: He provided an unsurpassed exemplar of civic and republican character.

He was a lawyer of great skill and integrity. He elevated and strengthened the administration of justice within the small towns and rural communities where he practiced. He fought eloquently against mob action wherever it erupted, whatever its purposes.

He was an activist from an early age. He began his political career as a local legislator, winning the votes of his fellow citizens, responding to their concerns, and earning their confidence. He then represented them briefly in Congress before returning to his home state.

He was a committed pluralist. Even as his political life became increasingly entangled with the intractable problem of slavery, he urged obedience to the Constitution. He tried to respect the constitutional prerogatives of the slaveholding states. He sought a peaceful evolution away from slaveholding, even as he worked to contain its occurrence within an increasingly small part of the nation.

As Lincoln strove to educate and persuade his fellow citizens, however, it became apparent that the Constitution's policy of tolerance and accommodation between the various states and regions was breaking down over slavery. He then sought the Presidency, won it, and used its emergency powers with great skill and determination. Finally he led the way in amending the

Constitution to prohibit the great sin against self-government that slavery represented.

It is hard to imagine a higher standard of republican citizenship than that set by Abraham Lincoln. He regarded the Constitution he inherited from his political forebears as a scripture — a political scripture, yes, but also a moral and cultural scripture. He did his utmost to meet its demands and honor its prohibitions. He was at the same time a very careful student of the ancient scripture of his people. He made frequent use of biblical language and imagery, moving the American people so powerfully that they were able to sustain a long and bloody war over slavery. At the peak of his career his rhetoric blended biblical and republican themes so beautifully that no clear or fundamental distinction remained. He became an American prophet, one whose visions were drawn from the Bible, the Declaration of Independence, and the Constitution.

Lincoln was surely not the first hero of civic republicanism. Among the American founders were a number. Students of the classical world will find a few as long ago as two and a half millennia. Perhaps the most outstanding was Socrates, who served his city in wartime; who spent his days reasoning with his fellow Athenians about justice and wisdom and the good life; and who chose to end his long life in obedience to a legal condemnation issued by a jury of his peers.

Article IV

Section 1. Full Faith and Credit shall be given in each State to the public Acts, Records, and judicial Proceedings of every other State; And the Congress may by general Laws prescribe the Manner in which such Acts, Records and Proceedings shall be proved, and the Effect thereof.

Section 2. The Citizens of each State shall be entitled to all Privileges and Immunities of Citizens in the several States.

A Person charged in any State with Treason, Felony, or other Crime, who shall flee from Justice, and be found in another State, shall on Demand of the executive Authority of the State from which he fled, be delivered up, to be removed to the State having Jurisdiction of the Crime.

[*No Person held to Service or Labour in one State, under the Laws thereof, escaping into another, shall, in Consequence of any Law or Regulation therein, be discharged from such Service or Labour, but shall be delivered up on Claim of the Party to whom such Service or Labour may be due.*]

Section 3. New States may be admitted by the Congress into this Union; but no new State shall be formed or erected within the Jurisdiction of any other State; nor any State be formed by the Junction of two or more States, or Parts of States, without the Consent of the Legislatures of the States concerned as well as of the Congress.

The Congress shall have Power to dispose of and make all needful Rules and Regulations respecting the Territory or other Property belonging to the United States; and nothing in this Constitution shall be so construed as to Prejudice any Claims of the United States, or of any particular State.

Section 4. The United States shall guarantee to every State in this Union a Republican Form of Government, and shall protect each of them against Invasion; and on Application of the Legislature, or of the Executive (when the Legislature cannot be convened) against domestic Violence.

Critics of the Constitution, pointing to the third paragraph of Section 2 and several related provisions, are quick to decry an outrageous affront to the principle of equality. Sometimes, in their indignation, they fail to mention the later deletion of the offensive language by the Civil War Amendments. And seldom do they remark how awkwardly the idea and the prac- tice of involuntary servitude fit within the text, even in 1787. In Article IV alone, the concession to the historical fact of slavery sat uneasily alongside several conflicting principles.

One was the guarantee to each state of a republican form of government.

Another appeared in the statement of two reciprocities, two forms of equality: one between citizens, another between local governments.

And more generally, throughout the Constitution, its authors shunned the word, slave, speaking rather of persons held. They went out of their way to taint the idea that a human being could legitimately be treated as property. Implicit in their diction was a tacit protest against the awkward position in which history had placed their new Republic.

Article V

The Congress, whenever two thirds of both Houses shall deem it necessary, shall propose Amendments to this Constitution, or, on the Application of the Legis- latures of two thirds of the several States, shall call a Convention for proposing Amendments, which, in either Case, shall be valid to all Intents and Purposes, as Part of this Constitution, when ratified by the Legislatures of three fourths of the several States, or by Conventions in three fourths thereof, as the one or the other Mode of ratification may be proposed by the Congress; Provided that no Amendment which may be made prior to the Year One thousand eight hundred and eight shall in any Manner affect the first and fourth Clauses in the Ninth Section of the first Article; and that no State, without its Consent, shall be deprived of its equal Suffrage in the Senate.

Here the governed, acting through their elected representatives, were given authority to amend the structures, methods, and purposes of their governance; an authority, moreover, not formally limited in any way. Here the many were given legal recourse against the few as to grievances felt widely and deeply enough. But change pursuant to this Article would not easily be made. Caution and prudence, to the constitutional authors, were very important political virtues.

All the more noteworthy in this context, then, is the suggestion that the abhorrent trade in human beings was in immediate danger of becoming the target of a constitutional amendment. Apparently the statesmen convened at Philadelphia in 1787 judged that slaveholding did not enjoy broad support among the American people. And the prompt prohibition of that trade by Congress twenty-one years later offers a telling indication that those gentlemen did not misread the public sentiment of their day.

Article VI

All Debts contracted and Engagements entered into, before the Adoption of this Constitution, shall be as valid against the United States under this Constitution, as under the Confederation.

This Constitution, and the Laws of the United States which shall be made in Pursuance thereof; and all Treaties made, or which shall be made, under the Authority of the United States, shall be the supreme Law of the Land; and the Judges in every State shall be bound thereby, any Thing in the Constitution or Laws of any State to the Contrary notwithstanding.

The Senators and Representatives before mentioned, and the Members of the several State Legislatures, and all executive and judicial Officers, both of the United States and of the several States, shall be bound by Oath or Affirmation, to support this Constitution; but no religious Test shall ever be required as a Qualification to any Office or public Trust under the United States.

Amidst what we might call several housekeeping provisions needed in a system of distinct but closely interrelated governments, two in particular stand out: the subordination of the laws of every state to those of the nation, and the exemption of officials of the nation's new central government from religious oaths.

Regarding the first: What might appear at first glance to be a program for gradual consolidation of authority in the new central government was really not. For only those laws of the nation properly authorized under the Constitution were to override local laws. The qualification was no mere gesture. There were many topics which the Constitution did not address and as to which Congress was to make no law. The formal distinction, and the tension between the local and the national, were both taken quite seriously — we might even say religiously — by early citizens of the United States. Generations of Americans would pay close attention to the constitutional language so carefully crafted by the statesmen of 1787 and 1791. Americans of that time did not confuse civic equality with legal or cultural identity.

The third paragraph also should be noted. The exemption of national officials from religious oaths looks back to two previous constitutional passages: the Preamble, where the relatively mundane character intended for the new central government was adumbrated; and Article I Section 8, where the meaning of "mundane" became a little clearer. This paragraph also prefigures a later development; for the noticeable absence of any exemption for state officials from religious oaths will resonate, four years later, with the first provision of the first constitutional amendment, not yet written or ratified in 1787.

Article VII

The Ratification of the Conventions of nine States, shall be sufficient for the Establishment of this Constitution between the States so ratifying the Same.

done in Convention by the Unanimous Consent of the States present the Seventeenth Day of September in the Year of our Lord one thousand seven hundred and Eighty seven and of the Independence of the United States of America the Twelfth, In Witness whereof We have hereunto subscribed our Names,

From this final article concerning the mode of ratification, the egalitarian spirit once more shines forth. Here some forty prominent representatives of the American aristocracy addressed themselves formally to the citizenry-at-large. They had labored together over a long, hot summer. Probably more than a few of them, far from home, were worried and distracted about their personal concerns. They had persevered in a tiring struggle to resolve serious differences of opinion. They had compromised as to important points and brought forth a text of some forty-four hundred words. Finally they were able to raise up this beacon of hope before the still fragile young nation.

And yet: They unhesitatingly submitted the result of this personally expensive and politically uncertain venture to the judgment, yea or nay, of hundreds of thousands of their fellow citizens, as expressed through thirteen local conventions.

The statesmen of 1787, that is, disciplined themselves to persuade. They did not try to domineer or overawe. Nor did they attempt to bind states whose citizens might reject the proposed new government. Communities unwilling to compromise their local independence would be allowed to stand apart.

Amendment I

Congress shall make no law respecting an establishment of religion, or prohibiting the free exercise thereof; or abridging the freedom of speech, or of the press, or the right of the people peaceably to assemble, and to petition the Government for a redress of grievances.

Article I Section 8 had been noticeably silent about various traditional concerns to which princes and parliaments had always addressed themselves. In the first sixteen words of the First Amendment, the negation of any general Congressional authority as to religion, left tacit in Article I Section 8, was expressly confirmed. In matters religious, in the realm of the sacred, any Congressional action would bear a stigma, presumptive if not conclusive, of constitutional transgression.

And the stigma was immediately broadened: Speech and the press, peaceable assemblies, and petitions of grievance were also not to be subjects of Congressional regulation.

Aren't these four prohibitions closely related? Speech and religion cannot be disentangled. Speech is the intercourse of souls, the spiritual commerce of individuals and communities. Through the circulating medium of words people come together in myriad relations, narrow and broad, transient and enduring, mundane and spiritual. An open and honest exchange of views and purposes is a potentially religious transaction; it is a ceremony performed before the altar of truth. Meetings, groups, assemblies, associations of all kinds, are the settings in which human beings most effectively engage one another and flourish. They are the natural habitat in which civic friendship and political activity and religious observance are born.

The First Amendment anointed each of its four named forms of interaction with a sacral character, so to speak. It made of them what we can fairly call civic sacraments.

What then about other omissions from Article I Section 8? "Congress shall have power to ..." surely implies, as to topics not listed, "Congress shall not have power to ..." The wording of Article I Section 8 erected a number of constitutional barriers behind which states and municipalities were to be protected against national dominance. Relations between the sexes, family life, education, property regulations, commercial ethics, the professions of medicine and law, literature and the arts come easily to mind here; also the suppression of common crimes. All these were implicitly identified as concerns not entrusted to the nation's legislature.

Did that place these local prerogatives also, in constitutional terms, within the realm of the sacred? Did it remove them from the realm of the mundane, making national legislation regarding them not merely inappropriate but constitutionally profane?

Here there is ambiguity. The topics not listed in Article I Section 8 can surely bear spiritual significance, but they also, and often, are very tangible and practical. They can touch the sense of the sacred in one way or another. By contrast, it seems a stretch to say that about the Congressional duty to establish a postal system, or to regulate the nation's commercial interactions with foreign peoples. We can best say, perhaps, that the Congressional responsibilities tend toward the mundane and pragmatic.

What we can say with confidence, however, is that the First Amendment highlights and emphasizes the theme of pluralism encountered in Article I Section 8. What may have appeared only as political pluralism in the earlier passage surely suggested, upon a close reading, religious pluralism also. With the First Amendment the suggestion becomes a pointed confirmation. The First Amendment, in emphasizing religious concerns so strongly, declared pluralism itself sacred. As to first things, as to ultimate concerns, unities and orthodoxies required of American citizens were to be the exception, not the rule.

Once we recognize the religious status to which the Constitution elevated pluralism, we are prompted to ask further: What other civic sacraments were embedded in the Constitution? And several come immediately to mind.

The legal order, the principle of treating like cases alike, was sanctified in Article I; as was the character of the law-respecting and law-abiding citizen.

Open and ongoing dialogue between elected lawmakers and their constituents was also sanctified in Article I, together with habits of active participation in public affairs.

Authority — power clothed in legitimacy, power dignified through lawful ascent to public offices — was sanctified in each of the first three Articles.

Reason, the use of reason to arbitrate across the wide spectrum of human conflict, was sanctified especially in Article III; but also throughout the Constitution.

* * *

We must be careful here. The Constitution pursued various purposes and used various methods. The specific assignment to Congress of particular responsibilities marked those subjects, presumptively, as appropriate for one rule and one way nationwide; it did not declare them of lesser rank. Congress was to attend to pressing public concerns, and to serious challenges to the good order and prosperity of the nation. Perhaps some of the matters assigned Congress were thought by the constitutional authors to invite less spiritual dissension. Perhaps some of those matters, even if they were spiritually sensitive, were thought nonetheless to require the pursuit of uniformity. On the other hand: The constitutional authors entrusted to the local governments indubitably sacred concerns, even as they left those same authorities many mundane concerns also.

The venerable concepts of sacred and profane designate spiritual extremes. When the Constitution commands, a civic sanctification is declared; when it proscribes, a civic profanation is implied. But though the Constitution sets forth a number of mandates and prohibitions, it also does much else. Where it is silent or ambiguous, we should hesitate. The sentiments which may tempt us to sanctify, or to anathematize, are too easily summoned; and once set loose, too difficult to placate.

Five constitutional sanctifications, five civic sacraments have been identified. These were considered essential components of republican government, in the judgment of the American founders. A republican form of government, moreover, was enjoined upon each of the local governments by Article IV Section 4.

And yet: Article V apparently allowed the people of the United States, should they become aggrieved enough and determined enough — and united enough in their grievances — to bring about, constitutionally, the dissolution of the Union, thereby putting an end to the Constitution. The Constitution's great cause and animating purpose is republican government; yet it can accommodate, within its four corners, the abolition of republican government.

This is counterintuitive, to say the least. Perhaps we should call it a mystery. Further, how can we expect the central government, oriented at it is toward mundane concerns, to bind together a vast nation encompassing a variety of faiths and creeds? Piety toward the same gods, some minimal but fundamental agreement as to sacred things, had always been thought essential to that purpose. To no small extent the American founders defied that historical consensus. Their legacy to the new nation included this perplexing novelty.

We cannot classify the culture or the government of the United States as either religious or secular. The culture was both religious and secular; unsurprisingly, then, that culture's elaborate system of government was both religious and secular. The formal assertion that millions of persons could join together and flourish amidst true religious pluralism — the implicit expectation that they would even flourish best when local communities were not bound to one interpretation of sacred things — was no "secular" stance.

This postulate or hypothesis — let us call it the American hypothesis — was derived from a European religious inheritance. European thinkers during the sixteenth and seventeenth centuries, amidst fierce and deadly struggles, had reluctantly concluded that the attempt to create spiritual uniformity by force was futile. Christian sectarianism had proven so destructive that the appalled and exhausted contenders finally settled for a policy of live and let live. The European settlement, however, emerging from a century and more of bloody struggles, was tentative and ad hoc. Americans of the eighteenth century, once they had won their independence, once they could enjoy a brief respite from political turbulence and warfare, promptly gave the policy a careful and articulate and constitutional form.

The legal commitment to religious pluralism is itself an article of faith. The conviction that human beings are capable of civic friendship even in the face of deep spiritual dissension is one reading of human nature, and probably not a common reading. Is such a remarkable confidence realistic? Profundity is no guarantee of validity. The American experiment represented a very bold leap into the future. The constitutional authors of 1787 and 1791 surely posed their political heirs some nice puzzles indeed. But they and their successors have left us several thousand more words to be considered.

Amendment II

A well regulated Militia, being necessary to the security of a free State, the right of the people to keep and bear Arms, shall not be infringed.

Five missing words — Congress shall make no law — will echo in the ears of the reader coming immediately to this Amendment from the first. The same five words could easily have qualified this prohibition also. The Amendment's authors thought it unnecessary to include them, or did not choose to do so. Did they intend thereby to limit the authority of the local governments also? Was this issue of arms and defense to be the business of the one city, the universal city, the nation? One way for all, or different ways for different communities?

And in addition to the intent of the constitutional authors, there is another pertinent consideration: Is the defense of self and family and community a sacred privilege and a solemn obligation?

Article I Section 8 allocated to Congress the authority to provided armed forces for defense of the nation. Article II empowered the President to direct that defense. Defending the nation must assuredly include defending each and every local community comprising the nation. But nothing was said in Articles I or II about the defense of individuals. Policing against crime, moreover, was clearly, in general, a function of the local governments; and reliance upon an armed constabulary of citizens is one method of meeting that responsibility.

If self-defense is a sacred right, then regulation of the individual use of arms is a form of religious legislation. This would put armed self-defense under the presumptive authority of the local governments, and therefore would insure a variety of regulatory approaches according to local circumstances. The civic sacrament of pluralism would thus be honored.

On the other hand: Could self-defense be reasonably understood as a merely mundane concern? Even if so, still, why would this override the lack of any mention of the topic in Article I Section 8? And surely the maintenance and control of a national military is not inconsistent with the private ownership of weapons by the nation's citizens.

Some ambiguity remained, perhaps. Points of future contention may not have been anticipated, or simply left to await future developments. But note that so far, in the constitutional text, the various curtailments of local authority had been clearly stated.

Amendment III

No Soldier shall, in time of peace be quartered in any house, without the consent of the Owner, nor in time of war, but in a manner to be prescribed by law.

Let us assume that the obligation to defend the United States against its enemies, explicitly assigned to Congress and to the President working together, is constitutionally sacred. If, by contrast, the right to control the use of one's property is constitutionally mundane, then there is no tension here. But isn't the latter right also ranked very high indeed?

A man's home is his castle: This is a venerable old maxim in the Anglo-American tradition.

Suppose we regard both the nation's obligation and the homeowner's right as constitutionally sacred. These can, and in some extreme circumstances will clash. A military commandeering of private property is at best a mundane business. To the victim of such an action it will likely seem profane. Carried out by an inept or brutal officer it will be profane. Yet such incidents may well be unavoidable in the course of a war. Here the constitutional authors empowered Congress to regulate the resulting conflicts as the nation's legislators should deem best.

Thus can a sharp conflict between two sacred concerns, under certain circumstances, generate a mundane necessity, or even a profane one.

Two centuries and more of mostly unbroken domestic peace have moved this amendment far toward the back of the public mind, but it furnishes a useful exercise in constitutional logic.

Amendment IV

The right of the people to be secure in their persons, houses, papers, and effects, against unreasonable searches and seizures, shall not be violated, and no Warrants shall issue, but upon probable cause, supported by Oath or affirmation, and particularly describing the place to be searched, and the persons or things to be seized.

Here we see the constitutional authors balancing opposing interests: a citizen suspected of crime, vis-à-vis the organized political community. And here again the missing five words prompt us to ask: Which organized political community? Is the central government the sole target of these restrictions? Or are the local governments to be similarly constrained?

Surely the preservation of a zone of personal security and peace of mind for each citizen qualifies as a constitutionally sacred public purpose. But so, just as surely, does the collective purpose of suppressing criminal activity.

The spiritual weight of this moral and political tension, then, suggests that its legal adjustment and regulation were intended in 1787 to be a prerogative of the local governments.

> Amendment V
>
> No person shall be held to answer for a capital, or otherwise infamous crime, unless on a presentment or indictment of a Grand Jury, except in cases arising in the land or naval forces, or in the Militia, when in actual service in time of War or public danger; nor shall any person be subject for the same offence to be twice put in jeopardy of life or limb, nor shall be compelled in any criminal case to be a witness against himself, nor be deprived of life, liberty, or property, without due process of law; nor shall private property be taken for public use without just compensation.

Here are no less than five protections for individual citizens at odds with public officials. Three are applicable only in criminal proceedings, one only in civil, and one in either type. And here again the missing five words seem to invite the recurring question: Which public officials, which government?

All these legal requirements are heavily weighted with moral and spiritual significance. Legislation focused upon them, whether in clarification or expansion or restriction, would seem therefore, presumptively, to be religious or quasi-religious legislation forbidden to Congress by the First Amendment. State legislatures, by contrast, would have been free to interpret and refine each of them under state law.

This Amendment offers also an oblique insight into the American law of property. The incidents of ownership received at this point their second mention in the Bill of Rights, both times only in reference to rather unusual circumstances. The general regulation of land, buildings, and other possessions was not among the powers given to the Congress in Article I Section 8. Property codes, therefore, would originate in the states and would be as numerous as the states. Private ownership, a key lever in the balance between individual and community, was left almost entirely under the control of the local governments. The meaning of mine versus thine, and the methods of distinguishing, were to be determined by many cities rather than one universal city. This was a central and fundamental expression of the American emphasis upon pluralism.

The widespread ownership of land and other goods, together with an open market, generates pervasive and energetic economic activity. Participants in such an economy will be recurrently trading with one another, bargaining with one another, working together in the mundane business of getting along. They will live the ethos of pluralism day by day, becoming accustomed to it and expecting to encounter it among others. Their daily lives will be filled with elementary observances of this civic sacrament; the character of which they will adjust, periodically, through their exercise of two other civic sacraments, those of electoral politics and law-making.

Amendment VI

> In all criminal prosecutions, the accused shall enjoy the right to a speedy and public trial, by an impartial jury of the State and district wherein the crime shall have been committed; which district shall have been previously ascertained by law, and to be informed of the nature and cause of the accusation; to be confronted with the witnesses against him; to have compulsory process for obtaining witnesses in his favor, and to have the assistance of counsel for his defence.

Seven more protections are added here for persons accused of crime. Again, the moral and spiritual weight of these tensions between individual and community is heavy indeed. Here again therefore, presumptively, the local governments would enjoy considerable latitude. Not one city, not one way only; rather many cities and many ways.

Amendment VII

> In Suits at common law, where the value in contro-
> versy shall exceed twenty dollars, the right of trial by
> jury shall be preserved, and no fact tried by a jury shall
> be otherwise re-examined in any Court of the United
> States, than according to the rules of the common law.

The focus shifts to civil proceedings, where juries — already mentioned in two prior Amendments — were also intended to play an important role. As a selection of impartial citizens representing the larger public, the jury is another egalitarian institution. In criminal cases the jurors can counter a judge's prestige and temper a prosecutor's zeal. In private suits they can bring to bear a broader perspective upon conflicting interests and purposes.

We do not need to be actually engaged in pleading a case to our peers to appreciate the importance, indeed the sanctity, of the right to do so. Such sacred concerns are presumably the province of the local governments, except as constitutionally mandated; a presumption strengthened in this Amendment by the reference to courts of the United States.

Thus again, despite the missing five words, the founding generation would have honored the civic sacrament of pluralism in their assumption that this Amendment governed the nation's courtrooms only.

Amendment VIII

> Excessive bail shall not be required, nor excessive fines
> imposed, nor cruel and unusual punishments inflicted.

With two words, excessive and cruel, this Amendment took on an overtly moral tone in confronting the danger of abusive governmental action. The weighty cultural and religious impli-cations of this prohibition, and the elusiveness of clear judgments as to what is excessive or cruel, were considered in the introduction to this book.

Here again, then, citizens of the early Republic would have understood this admonition and restriction to be addressed to the central government only.

Amendment IX

The enumeration in the Constitution of certain rights shall not be construed to deny or disparage others retained by the people.

Now comes a sharp change in perspective. Turning from particular principles bearing upon the administration of justice, we find ourselves contemplating justice itself, the meaning and the origin of justice. The nation's judges have been hesitant to cite this Amendment, and surely that is understandable. Some students of the Constitution consider it an expression of legal mysticism. Its application to a specific case or controversy invites all-too-plausible accusations of judicial invention or legislation. But it has sometimes been cited.

One possible interpretation: The previous eight Amendments articulated a number of rights. Implicit in the constitutional text of 1787, however, are other rights, individual and communal. Could the intended reference of the Ninth Amendment, in 1791, have been those rights already vested in the people of the United States by the ratification of the Constitution in 1789?

Then again, this Amendment may have signified in the minds of its authors a law independent of human action, a law not arising from the speech of any tongue nor the writing of any hand; but a binding law nonetheless, although few, or none, can state it fully or define it with precision. This Amendment may have been suggesting that there are laws given us, along with our lives, by nature or by divinity.

The Ninth Amendment, that is, might point toward the ancient doctrine of natural right, or natural law. This would not have been troubling to the constitutional authors, nor to several succeeding generations of American jurists and lawyers. But the idea became highly controversial in the twentieth century, and remains so to the present.

Amendment X

The powers not delegated to the United States by the Constitution, nor prohibited by it to the States, are reserved to the States respectively, or to the people.

The importance of this Amendment is suggested by its placement. It culminates the initial set of ten Amendments, adopted in 1791 in fulfilment of political promises which facilitated the state-by-state ratification of the Constitution. Nothing, moreover, suggests that the principle it proclaims is any less applicable to such Amendments as may be added later. Here the theme adumbrated by the Preamble, the same theme then suggested more fully in Article I Section 8, is reiterated and given added force: The nation's government, the central government, is intended to be a partial government, a truncated sovereign authority. Very frequently the nation's central government should defer, as a matter of principle, to the decisions and policies of the various local governments.

It is no exaggeration to describe the Tenth Amendment as foundational. It should never be far from the minds of Senators and Representatives and Presidents; nor, especially, of the nation's Judges. It must inform any sound approach to constitutional reasoning. It does not purport to create constitutional rights; rather, it prescribes a principle by which to test those rights, and if necessary to clarify them, when inconsistencies are alleged.

In the American nation, says the Tenth Amendment, local communities too are to be regarded as citizens.

There is a historical resonance here. If human beings are by nature political beings, then they seek fulfillment in a political life. They need what the Greeks called a polis. But a polis, if it extends its sway too far, must become an empire. The citizens of an extensive empire will not long remain citizens, they will become subjects. They will cease to be participants in their own governance.

Thus was the American republic designed to achieve a complex balance. The tensions between individuals and communities would often be adjusted by the interplay of various officials of at least two governments. Those adjustments could be tested in the courts of the nation for compatibility with the principles and standards set forth in the Constitution. The judicial adjustments could then in turn be tested in Congress. Multiple paths and settings were provided for the resolution of conflict. So long as this elaborate plan worked as intended, the United States could hardly become a monoculture, either political or social.

Seven of the nine previous Amendments, in itemizing restraints upon governmental action, had left unstated which government or governments were being restrained. The Tenth Amendment supplied that omission. Although it provides no answer to any specific controversy between national and local officials, it prescribes the rule which is to guide such deliberations. The national authorities are not to displace the local unless the constitutional text cogently points to that conclusion. Amendment X left no doubt as to which pattern was to be the American norm: many cities rather than one universal city, many ways rather than one way.

This preference for diversity, this prejudice against uniformity, was tested and confirmed in the nation's Supreme Court in 1833. On that occasion the Justices, led by the first great Chief Justice, John Marshall, unanimously declined to allow a citizen of Maryland to invoke the Fifth Amendment in support of his grievances against the City of Baltimore.[14] Marshall explained briefly and clearly why the Bill of Rights, in contrast to various provisions of the constitutional text, had not been intended by the founding generation to curtail the authority of local governments. And twelve years later, in a First Amendment

---

[14] Barron v. City of Baltimore, 32 U.S. 243 (1833)

case brought against the City of New Orleans, the Court, again unanimously, adhered to the 1833 precedent.[15]

Amendment XI

> The Judicial power of the United States shall not be construed to extend to any suit in law or equity, commenced or prosecuted against one of the United States by Citizens of another State, or by Citizens or Subjects of any Foreign State.

An early adjustment. When a citizen of one state filed suit in a national court against the government of a different state seeking enforcement of a contract — and when the suit was allowed to proceed by the Supreme Court — Congress promptly submitted this Amendment to the states. It was promptly ratified. Although the local governments were to be citizens of the Republic, they were not quite ordinary citizens. As quasi-sovereign authorities, they would enjoy certain prerogatives not allowed individuals.

This first refinement of the egalitarian ideal heralded others to come — a number of them too momentous and consequential to be called adjustments.

Amendment XII

> The Electors shall meet in their respective states, and vote by ballot for President and Vice President, one of whom, at least, shall not be an inhabitant of the same state with themselves; they shall name in their ballots the person voted for as President, and in distinct ballots the person voted for as Vice-President, and they shall make distinct lists of all persons voted for as President, and of all persons voted for as Vice-President, and of the number of votes for each, which lists they shall sign and certify, and transmit sealed

---

[15] Permoli v. City of New Orleans, 44 U.S. 589 (1845)

to the seat of the government of the United States, directed to the President of the Senate; — The President of the Senate shall, in the presence of the Senate and House of Representatives, open all the certificates and the votes shall then be counted; — The person having the greatest number of votes for President, shall be the President, if such number be a majority of the whole number of Electors appointed; and if no person have such majority, then from the persons having the highest numbers not exceeding three on the list of those voted for as President, the House of Representatives shall choose immediately, by ballot, the President. But in choosing the President, the votes shall be taken by states, the representation from each state having one vote; a quorum for this purpose shall consist of a member or members from two-thirds of the states, and a majority of all the states shall be necessary to a choice. [*And if the House of Representatives shall not choose a President whenever the right of choice shall devolve upon them, before the fourth day of March next following, then the Vice-President shall act as President, as in the case of the death or other constitutional disability of the President* —] The person having the greatest number of votes as Vice-President, shall be the Vice-President, if such number be a majority of the whole number of Electors appointed, and if no person have a majority, then from the two highest numbers on the list, the Senate shall choose the Vice-President; a quorum for the purpose shall consist of two-thirds of the whole number of Senators, and a majority of the whole number shall be necessary to a choice. But no person constitutionally ineligible to the office of President shall be eligible to that of Vice-President of the United States.

The elaborate procedures for selection of the nation's chief executive were soon found vulnerable to serious complications. The changes set forth here retained the complexity, but preserved the principle that ascent to the most powerful office in the nation's government was to be tested and confirmed by many distinct electorates and subordinate officials. Direct democracy had few advocates in the early Republic.

Amendment XIII

Section 1. Neither slavery nor involuntary servitude, except as a punishment for crime whereof the party shall have been duly convicted, shall exist within the United States, or any place subject to their jurisdiction.

Section 2. Congress shall have power to enforce this article by appropriate legislation.

Intimidation and coercion are crude forms of inequality. Violence is even cruder; and, except in narrow or extreme circumstances, a crime. Intimidation, coercion, and violence, officially perpetrated in support of slavery, become a general and public crime. But slavery was widely practiced throughout the ancient, the medieval and the early modern world, and it could be found in all the British colonies in North America.

With the costly sacrifices of the Civil War having purchased the Republic a new latitude of action, civic equality could finally receive this forceful endorsement and begin to play a larger role in the life of the nation. Under this Amendment and the two which followed quickly upon it, involuntary servitude was declared a constitutional profanity, the inverse of the liberty framed by the Preamble as a central purpose of the Union. With this Amendment slaveholding could no longer be treated as a mundane and optional concern anywhere in the nation. With this Amendment, equality could assume its rightful place among the other ideals listed in the Preamble to the Constitution.

These legal measures, of course, in themselves, could not possibly integrate former slaves into the larger society upon fair, let alone generous terms. Their symbolic importance and their practical effect were immense, but slavery's legacy of fear and hatred could be purged only gradually.

Note also the appearance here of the first explicit recognition of Congressional responsibility for implementation. This reiteration of the principle of legislative primacy was itself an offering laid upon the altar of equality. The measures to be taken to secure the new freedom were to be supported by a formal popular consensus. The sacrament of active civic participation was intended to inform and direct the nation's pursuit of a more egalitarian future.

Amendment XIV

Section 1. All persons born or naturalized in the United States and subject to the jurisdiction thereof, are citizens of the United States and of the State wherein they reside. No State shall make or enforce any law which shall abridge the privileges or immunities of citizens of the United States; nor shall any State deprive any person of life, liberty, or property, without due process of law; nor deny to any person within its jurisdiction the equal protection of the laws.

Section 2. Representatives shall be apportioned among the several States according to their respective numbers, counting the whole number of persons in each State, excluding Indians not taxed. But when the right to vote at any election for the choice of electors for President and Vice President of the United States, Representatives in Congress, the Executive and Judicial officers of a State, or the members of the Legislature thereof, is denied to any of the male inhabitants of such State, being twenty-one years of age, and citizens of the United States, or in any way abridged, except for participation in rebellion, or other crime, the basis of representation therein shall be reduced in the proportion which the number of such male citizens shall bear to the whole number of male citizens twenty-one years of age in such State.

Section 3. No person shall be a Senator or Representative in Congress, or elector of President and Vice President, or hold any office, civil or military, under the United States, or under any State, who, having previously taken an oath, as a member of Congress, or as an officer of the United states, or as a member of any State legislature, or as an executive or judicial officer of any State, to support the Constitution of the United States, shall have engaged in insurrection or rebellion against the same, or given aid or comfort to the enemies thereof. But Congress may by a vote of two-thirds of each House, remove such disability.

Section 4. The validity of the public debt of the United States, authorized by law, including debts incurred for payment of pensions and bounties for services in suppressing insurrection or rebellion, shall not be questioned. But neither the United States nor any state shall assume or pay any debt or obligation incurred in aid of insurrection or rebellion against the United States, or any claim for the loss or emancipation of any slave; but all such debts, obligations and claims shall be held illegal and void.

Section 5. The Congress shall have power to enforce, by appropriate legislation, the provisions of this article.

In the previous Amendment the ideal of civic equality had received a vehement but negative endorsement — the prohibition of its grossest violation. The first section of the present Amendment recognizes the inadequacy of bare anathema to bring word and deed into alignment. The requisite positive guidance, however, is quite carefully stated. The equality described is legal equality, or civic equality: equal privileges and immunities, equal treatment by the laws, and fair process in legal proceedings. Laws implementing these three principles can well leave a good deal of room for individual and local initiative; and, therefore, a good deal of room for inequalities among people of widely varying backgrounds, aptitudes, interests, and energies. The authors of this Amendment cannot be plausibly accused of seeking a comprehensive equality among Americans.

But then, what might "comprehensive equality" mean? Can anyone explain intelligibly how that might work?

Again, with the last section of this Amendment, the nation's legislators were reminded of their responsibility to put flesh on the egalitarian bones. The great goal of civic equality was to be pursued through the observance of two foundational civic equalities, two civic sacraments: the enactment of laws, by elected representatives.

There is no warrant here, that is, for government by edict.

Amendment XV

Section 1. The right of citizens of the United States to vote shall not be denied or abridged by the United States or by any State on account of race, color, or previous condition of servitude.

Section 2. The Congress shall have power to enforce this article by appropriate legislation.

The statesmen who brought an intact nation through the Civil War were not content to rest the foundational privileges of American citizenship solely upon the expression given them in the two previous Amendments. Therefore persons once enslaved, now emancipated, received here a very specific constitutional guarantee of their right to participate in lawmaking at all levels of government.

And with that guarantee, again, came the reminder that legislators were primarily responsible for making it good. Elected officials were to lead the way in observing and celebrating the electoral sacrament.

Amendment XVI

The Congress shall have power to lay and collect taxes on incomes, from whatever source derived, without apportionment among the several states, and without regard to any census or enumeration.

In augmenting the revenues of the nation's central government, the constitutional authors of 1913 apparently considered civic equality a lesser concern. And indeed, soon enough, different rates for different taxpayers were set. No significant injustice was seen in having the middle class and the wealthy fund their government almost entirely, while those with small incomes were taxed little or not at all. Legislators, presumably with the approval of voters, gradually established an inverted hierarchy — the disadvantaged on top — to counterbalance the privileges of affluence.

Was this attempt to redress one inequality with a compensating inequality effective? Did it represent a sound understanding of economics? Of the egalitarian ideal? Of human nature?

These are difficult questions. But we can reasonably suspect that had this Amendment's authors chosen to require one income tax rate for all, our lives today, private and public, would be different, perhaps quite different.

Amendment XVII

The Senate of the United States shall be composed of two Senators from each State, elected by the people thereof, for six years; and each Senator shall have one vote. The electors in each State shall have the qualifications requisite for electors of the most numerous branch of the State legislatures.

When vacancies happen in the representation of any State in the Senate, the executive authority of such State shall issue writs of election to fill such vacancies: Provided, That the legislature of any State may empower the executive thereof to make temporary appointments until the people fill the vacancies by election as the legislature may direct.

This amendment shall not be so construed as to affect the election or term of any Senator chosen before it becomes valid as part of the Constitution.

The sacrament of civic dialogue, the procedures for grounding legislation in the will of citizens, received here an adjustment. Henceforth the nation's Senators too, not just its Representatives, would be elected directly, without the intermediation of local legislators.

Among the justifications put forward for the indirect election of Senators, and for their longer terms, had been the idea that they would tend thereby to be a seasoned group of elder statesmen; and that they might be not only inclined to moderate the political tempests which occasionally roil large numbers of people, but capable of doing so. This can be reasonably questioned. Perhaps demagogues can ply their trade as effectively among veteran politicians as they do among the populace at large.

Did this change actually advance the cause of civic equality?

Who knows? Here we are peering into the murkier precincts of the political life.

Amendment XVIII

[*Section 1. After one year from the ratification of this article the manufacture, sale, or transportation of intoxicating liquors within, the importation thereof into, or the exportation thereof from the United States and all territory subject to the jurisdiction thereof for beverage purposes is hereby prohibited.*

Section 2. The Congress and the several States shall have concurrent power to enforce this article by appropriate legislation.

Section 3. This article shall be inoperative unless it shall have been ratified as an amendment to the Constitution by the legislatures of the several States, as provided in the Constitution, within seven years from the date of the submission hereof to the states by the Congress.]

This was not the first attempt in the United States to bring order out of a messy and divisive array of laws and policies and practices. The reader will recall that the Supreme Court had attempted something similar in 1857, thus playing more than a small part in the onset of the Civil War. But the starring role in the first act of this drama over alcoholic beverages belonged to generations of sober and earnest American activists, who finally persuaded several hundred Congressmen to submit this Amendment, and thousands of local legislators to ratify it.

The second act featured the broader populace; who, fourteen years later, having seen enough of the new law's results, reversed course and returned the entire subject to the constitutional precincts where the founders had placed it — the local governments.

This supposed reform was radically out of character at the time, a flagrant departure from the accustomed ways of American history, politics, and law. The sacrament of civic pluralism was here trampled underfoot. Many thousands of pages of state and municipal legislation, the product of an immense expenditure of local political energy over a long time, a legal inheritance quite heterogeneously adapted to local mores and local circumstances, was suddenly swept away in a flash. Suddenly every village, every town, every city, every state in the nation was given one very simple and uncompromising mandate.

The Amendment was cleared by Congress and submitted to the states amidst the pressures and confusions generated by the nation's entry into the great European war raging in 1917. It was ratified in 1919 and became effective in 1920.

Note the first appearance here of a limited time for ratification — a telling sign that many Congressmen were uncomfortable with this piece of constitutional handiwork.

Little knowledge of American history is required to be aware of the multifaceted disaster that followed upon this effort to cleanse society, at one stroke, immediately and uniformly and peremptorily, of a troublesome social problem.

Amendment XIX

The right of citizens of the United States to vote shall
not be denied or abridged by the United States or by
any State on account of sex.

The Congress shall have power to enforce this article
by appropriate legislation.

With this Amendment, as with the one previous to it, came
sudden, sweeping, nationwide change. With this Amendment,
the electoral irrelevance of half the nation's citizens, a political
demarcation only relatively recently brought into question, was
ended. To describe this as an egalitarian measure is to under-
state its significance.

Yet, for all that, this was still a cautiously measured advance.
Note the careful and concise language. Local governments were
not instructed to rummage through their laws reassessing each
legal distinction between the sexes found there. Local legislation was left free to evolve along with the mores and judgments
of the governed. Only the act of participating in public elections
was comprehensively disencumbered of the weight of tradition
and prejudice. Further advances along this line were left to be
implemented at the local level.

That is to say: The principle of many cities, rather than one
universal and uniform city, was subtly but clearly honored in the
Nineteenth Amendment. The contemptuous rejection of that
principle in the Eighteenth Amendment sufficiently explains
why the earlier appears in retrospect as not only bad public
policy, but as a foolish and destructive exercise in utopian zeal;
while the Nineteenth is almost universally regarded as a simple
statement of democratic principle.

And indeed, the sudden enfranchisement of women provoked
little if any evasion or resistance.

Amendment XX

Section 1. The terms of the President and Vice President shall end at noon on the 20th day of January, and the terms of Senators and Representatives at noon on the 3d day of January, of the years in which such terms would have ended if this article had not been ratified; and the terms of their successors shall then begin.

Section 2. The Congress shall assemble at least once in every year, and such meeting shall begin at noon on the 3d day of January, unless they shall by law appoint a different day.

Section 3. If, at the time fixed for the beginning of the term of the President, the President elect shall have died, the Vice President elect shall become President. If a President shall not have been chosen before the time fixed for the beginning of his term, or if the President elect shall have failed to qualify, then the Vice President elect shall act as President until a President shall have qualified; and the Congress may by law provide for the case wherein neither a President elect nor a Vice President elect shall have qualified, declaring who shall then act as President, or the manner in which one who is to act shall be selected, and such person shall act accordingly until a President or Vice President shall have qualified.

Section 4. The Congress may by law provide for the case of the death of any of the persons from whom the House of Representatives may choose a President whenever the right of choice shall have devolved upon them, and for the case of the death of any of the persons from whom the Senate may choose a Vice President whenever the right of choice shall have devolved upon them.

Section 5. Sections 1 and 2 shall take effect on the 15th day of October following the ratification of this article.

Section 6. This article shall be inoperative unless it shall have been ratified as an amendment to the Constitution by the legislatures of three-fourths of the several States, as provided in the Constitution, within seven years from the date of its submission.

Another exercise in governmental housekeeping. The time-tables of an earlier age were here adapted to much more mobile and faster-moving ways of life. Some contingencies not previously or not clearly addressed also received attention.

Amendment XXI

Section 1. The eighteenth article of amendment to the Constitution of the United States is hereby repealed.

Section 2. The transportation or importation into any State, Territory, or possession of the United States for delivery or use therein of intoxicating liquors, in violation of the laws thereof, is hereby prohibited.

Section 3. This article shall be inoperative unless it shall have been ratified as an amendment to the Constitution by conventions in the several States, as provided in the Constitution, within seven years from the date of its submission hereof to the States by the Congress.

A democratic repentance. Here authority over alcoholic beverages — the very authority so unwisely usurped by the Eighteenth Amendment — was returned to the local governments. This dramatic tribute to the wisdom of 1787 is today lamentably forgotten.

Amendment XXII

Section 1. No person shall be elected to the office of the President more than twice, and no person who has held the office of President, or acted as President, for more than two years of a term to which some other person was elected President shall be elected to the office of the President more than once. But this Article shall not apply to any person holding the office of President when this Article was proposed by the Congress, and shall not prevent any person who may be holding he office of President, or acting as President, during the term within which this Article becomes operative from holding the office of President or acting as President during the remainder of such term.

Section 2. This article shall be inoperative unless it shall have been ratified as an amendment to the Constitution by the legislatures of three-fourths of the several States within seven years from the date of its submission to the States by the Congress.

Do we see in this a posthumous rebuke to a President considered by many to have held the office too long? Do we see the people of the United States chastising themselves here, as in the previous Amendment?

Or perhaps this Amendment addresses an ambiguity lurking in the abstract ideal of political equality. On the one hand, equality seems to be neglected or diminished by very lengthy tenures in office. Aristocracy, or oligarchy, might seem to threaten. On the other hand: Shouldn't equal citizens, as voters, be entitled to renew the term of a favored official as often as they wish?

Amendment XXIII

Section 1. The District constituting the seat of Government of the United States shall appoint in such manner as the Congress may direct:

A number of electors of President and Vice President equal to the whole number of Senators and Representatives in Congress to which the District would be entitled if it were a State, but in no event more than the least populous State; they shall be in addition to those appointed by the States, but they shall be considered, for the purposes of the election of President and Vice President, to be electors appointed by a State; and they shall meet in the District and perform such duties as provided by the twelfth article of amendment.

Section 2. The Congress shall have power to enforce this article by appropriate legislation.

Continuing growth in the District of Columbia resulted eventually in an awkward civic inequality — a significant number of citizens whose votes played no role in the appointment of Presidential electors. Here the problem was addressed.

Amendment XXIV

Section 1. The right of citizens of the United States to vote in any primary or other election for President or Vice President, for electors for President or Vice President, or for Senator or Representative in Congress, shall not be denied or abridged by the United States or any State by reason of failure to pay any poll tax or other tax.

Section 2. The Congress shall have power to enforce this article by appropriate legislation.

Another effort to promote civic equality. Conditioning the right to vote upon even a nominal monetary payment came to be seen as an unfair obstacle to the poorest voters, or an affront to their dignity; or perhaps both.

Amendment XXV

Section 1. In case of the removal of the President from office or of his death or resignation, the Vice President shall become President.

Section 2. Whenever there is a vacancy in the office of the Vice President, the President shall nominate a Vice president who shall take office upon confirmation by a majority vote of both Houses of Congress.

Section 3. Whenever the President transmits to the President pro tempore of the Senate and the Speaker of the House of Representatives his written declaration that he is unable to discharge the powers and duties of his office, and until he transmits to them a written declaration to the contrary, such powers and duties shall be discharged by the Vice President as Acting President.

Section 4. Whenever the Vice President and a majority of either the principal officers of the executive departments or of such other body as Congress may by law provide, transmit to the President pro tempore of the Senate and the Speaker of the House of Representatives their written declaration that the President is unable to discharge the powers and duties of his office, the Vice President shall immediately assume the powers and duties of the office as Acting President.

Thereafter, when the President transmits to the President pro tempore of the Senate and the Speaker of the House of Representatives his written declaration that no inability exists, he shall resume the powers and duties of his office unless the Vice President and a majority of either the principal officers of the executive departments or of such other body as Congress may by law provide, transmit within four days to the

President pro tempore of the Senate and the Speaker of the House of Representatives their written declaration that the President is unable to discharge the powers and duties of his office. Thereupon Congress shall decide the issue, assembling within forty-eight hours for that purpose if not in session. If the Congress, within twenty-one days after receipt of the latter written declaration, or, if Congress is not in session, within twenty-one days after Congress is required to assemble, determines by two-thirds vote of both Houses that the President is unable to discharge the powers and duties of his office, the Vice President shall continue to discharge the same as Acting President; otherwise, the President shall resume the powers and duties of his office.

A specter haunts the dreams of those devoted to the American Republic: the possibility of an unstructured struggle for power at the very highest levels of the nation's central government. But we have to ask: If the once-general reverence for the Constitution has slipped sufficiently to invite a political free-for-all, can the kind of fine tuning attempted in this Amendment provide a remedy?

Amendment XXVI

Section 1. The right of citizens of the United States, who are eighteen years of age or older, to vote shall not be denied or abridged by the United States or by any State on account of age.

Section 2. The Congress shall have power to enforce this article by appropriate legislation.

Another offering upon the altar of equality. "Old enough to fight, old enough to vote," said proponents of this Amendment. The idea that civic equality sometimes requires uniformity receives here a narrow but significant specification.

Amendment XXVII

No law, varying the compensation for the services of Representatives and Senators, shall take effect, until an election of Representatives shall have intervened.

This Amendment, ratified in 1992, is a historical curiosity. It was submitted to the thirteen original states by the First Congress in 1791, along with eleven other Amendments, ten of which were promptly ratified and became the Bill of Rights. This one was not ratified; rather it was forgotten and ignored for nearly two hundred years. Then a student of the Constitution noticed it and could find no reason why the long lapse of time should have nullified any earlier ratifications or should rule out later ratifications. He led a successful effort to publicize and promote it.

The Amendment is also a political curiosity. All previous Amendments required the expenditure of contemporaneous political labor at both the national and local levels; whereas the Congress which produced this one had been dissolved and replaced for two centuries by the time it was ratified. The most recent Amendment ratified during the political careers of the Senators and Representatives who authored it was the Twenty-Sixth, taking effect in 1971.

Thus for half a century now, no constitutional change has originated in Congress or been drafted and set in motion by the local governments.

Yet the pace of constitutional change has not slowed; if anything, it has accelerated. It seems that less formal and more expeditious methods of amendment than Article V have been found.

Let us now consider several more instances of the Supreme Court's exercises in constitutional revision.

CHAPTER FIVE: CONSCIENCE

In 1785 James Madison, who would play a leading role two years later at the constitutional convention in Philadelphia, drafted a "Memorial and Remonstrance," setting down some of his thoughts about the sensitive issue of religious liberty. The document was published as a protest against the efforts of Patrick Henry, another leader of the American Revolution, to obtain state funding for ministers of the various Protestant denominations in Virginia. Madison and his friends defeated Henry's bill, and thereby set the stage for the Virginia legislature's enactment in 1786 of a very different approach to the topic: Thomas Jefferson's "A Bill for Establishing Religious Freedom in Virginia."

Today's reader, pondering Madison's words, will find there some very striking propositions.

Religion, says Madison, is "the duty which we owe to our Creator and the manner of discharging it."

Religion, he says, can be directed only by reason and conviction, and must be left to the conviction and conscience of every man.

It is the right of every man, he says, to exercise his religious duties as his conviction and his conscience dictate.

Religious duties, he says, are precedent, both in order of time and in degree of obligation, to the claims of civil society; and are wholly exempt from the cognizance of civil society.

A just government, he says, will protect equally the religious rights of every sect, and will prevent any sect from invading the religious rights of another.

This is a bold program for religious liberty indeed! But surely we must ask: Can the five principles just stated really keep good company together through all the flux and the tensions of civic life? It is hardly clear that they can. Certainly the world's many religions and sects have shown themselves, throughout history, frequently incapable of coexisting peacefully.

Be that as it may, two features of Madison's thought are of special interest here: the close linkage which he sees between the human conscience and Divinity, and the extraordinary status he accords our duties to Divinity.

As to the first: Let us say that for Madison, when we consult our consciences, we are looking upward and outward. We raise our eyes toward the creator and lawgiver of the cosmos.

As for the second, the question of priority: Religious illumination and obligation, says Madison, flow downward. Our civic principles are to be interpreted and our civic arrangements adjusted in accordance with what is highest and best in us. The sacred must override the profane, obviously, but also the merely pragmatic or expedient.

Several Supreme Court rulings handed down in the twentieth century make very interesting reading in light of these reflections of Mr. Madison. We can find there some considerable wavering among his political heirs, as they try to focus the gaze of conscience.

* * *

In 1937, a man convicted of murder and scheduled for execution pled for his life before the Supreme Court of the United States. He complained of the manner in which the State of Connecticut had tried his case. His counsel's arguments were not, ultimately, persuasive to the Court, but the circumstances were admittedly unusual. He had been through two trials for his commission of one homicide.

Convicted the first time, he had been sentenced to life imprisonment. At the initial trial, however, some of the state's evidence against him had been excluded by the judge. The decision to keep that evidence from the jury moved his aggrieved prosecutors to appeal the jury's verdict; and the result was a retrial, in which the state was allowed to present its more complete case. At that second trial, moreover, the prosecution succeeded not only in convicting the accused, but also in convincing a new jury that his crime called for capital punishment.

Counsel for the condemned man probably expected to get the death sentence nullified. He had several reasons for optimism. For one, in contrast to so many constitutional litigations, here no one needed to search the founding charter for something directly applicable. In 1791, Congress had included in the Bill of Rights a prohibition of what came to be called double jeopardy: "... nor shall any person be subject for the same offense to be twice put in jeopardy of life or limb..." The accused had alleged double jeopardy in the Connecticut courts as soon as the local prosecutors appealed; but there his protest was unavailing. Convicted the second time, and having exhausted his state appeals, he then turned to the courts of the nation.

Further, although the Bill of Rights had originally forbidden only certain actions by the nation's central government, by the 1930s the Justices had begun to apply selected provisions of it against the state governments as well. Their rationale for doing so was one of the Civil War Amendments, the Fourteenth, which authorized national review and correction of state actions found to have denied someone due process of law. The Fourteenth Amendment, according to the Justices, had endowed certain legal safeguards with a greater weight, great enough to override conflicting local codes and practices.

Finally, and most encouraging for the appellant, the Supreme Court had already ruled, several decades earlier, that prosecutors in a criminal proceeding in one of the nation's courts could not, merely upon the government's claim that the trial judge had committed procedural errors, have a second chance at the accused.

So, if due process of law in the national courts would have forbidden prosecutors an appeal in the convicted man's unusual circumstances, why would the same rule not apply in the state courts? His chances of avoiding execution in 1937 must have seemed quite good.

Yet he stayed on death row. The Supreme Court decided that the State of Connecticut had not placed him twice in jeopardy — not, that is, in the constitutional sense, the sense forbidden by the Fifth Amendment.[16]

* * *

The outcome of this case might seem somewhat puzzling. The Justices' deference to the State of Connecticut might have suggested to them a reconsideration of the precedent which had governed criminal proceedings at the national level for several decades. They could have changed the rule in the nation's courts, in recognition of the ambiguities inherent in the controversy. But they did not do that.

Why? What seemed more important to the Justices than uniformity in criminal procedure?

They began by pointing out that the federal precedent in question had been a close decision, with the dissenting Justices presenting a very cogent concern. It is no light matter, the earlier dissenters had said, to allow a trial judge the power to release a dangerous criminal by mistakenly preventing prosecutors from properly presenting all the relevant evidence. But the majority at that time had been persuaded that justice was better served by running that risk. Hence the rule as it stood in the nation's courts in 1937.

The Justices also pointed out that the Connecticut legislature had enacted a statute specifically allowing state prosecutors the right to appeal alleged trial court errors in criminal proceedings. At least one local legislature, that is, obviously did not want potentially dangerous criminals being released due to caprice

---

[16] Palko v. State of Connecticut, 302 U.S. (1937)

or poor judgment or bias on the part of lower court judges. Presumably, that legislative judgment reflected the opinion of Connecticut's citizens as well. The people of Connecticut, through their representatives, had given formal expression — perhaps in light of some recent miscarriage of justice in that jurisdiction — to a policy of allowing a more adequate power of prosecution. Connecticut citizens had sought to establish a better balance between two sacred concerns: fairness to those accused of crime, yes, but also the need for effective public action against criminals.

Faced with these two public articulations of the sacred, counterpoised in tension with one another by highly unusual circumstances, the Justices declined to attempt a uniform and comprehensive adjustment.

The Connecticut statute, they said, did not offend against "... the very essence of a scheme of ordered liberty."

"The legislative judgment, if oppressive and arbitrary, may be overridden by the courts," they said; but they did not consider that to be the case here.

Regarding the idea that the power of a state government was overwhelmingly disproportionate to that of an accused individual, they said "A reciprocal privilege [of appeal] ... has now been granted to the state. ... The edifice of justice stands, its symmetry greater, to many, than before."

Implored for mercy, they replied that "This is not cruelty at all, nor even vexation in any immoderate degree."

They declined, in other words, to hold that a right of appeal for the government in criminal prosecutions violated any "principle of justice so rooted in the traditions and the conscience of our people as to be ranked as fundamental." They weighed the erroneous handicapping of the prosecution in the first trial against the hardship and peril suffered by the accused in undergoing a second, and they judged that the balance had been reasonable enough.

The Court judged, in effect, that here it had taken two attempts to get one fair trial; fair, that is, to the accused, to the prosecution, and therefore to the public. The Justices reviewed their own precedents and their nation's history, as well as the passages of constitutional text they thought relevant, and pronounced a judgment of conscience on behalf of the nation. The ideas of fairness and good conscience lay at the heart of this controversy. But the eighteenth-century authors of the Constitution and the Bill of Rights did not make use of those particular words. The reader may well ask, therefore, how the Constitution could have offered the Justices any real guidance. The terse constitutional orthodoxy on double jeopardy required further elucidation. But further elucidation by what?

Were the Justices left on their own, with nothing to do but to search their souls?

* * *

They were not. The Justices of 1937 overlooked important constitutional clues. For one thing, they displayed a new and troubling tendency to neglect Article I Section 8, which had deliberately left the primary responsibility for policing and punishing crime at the state level. In addition, in referring to the Bill of Rights, they spoke only of Amendments One through Eight. No careful student of American history would do that. Two of those neglected provisions, Article I Section 8 and the Tenth Amendment, were quite relevant to the case before them. Both Article I Section 8 and the Tenth Amendment made clear that the American soul, or the American conscience, had not been surrendered to the new central government in 1787. The Tenth Amendment made clear that in general, American citizens were to participate in decisions touching the public conscience. The Tenth Amendment offered instruction to future generations against an error — the error of routinely expecting the United States to speak with one voice — where the Constitution does not clearly call for unanimity.

Both Article I and the Tenth Amendment, ignored by the Justices of 1937, weighed against the Court's overriding of the state statute addressing the conscionability of prosecutorial appeals. Article I and the Tenth Amendment offer valuable guidance where urgent but incompatible concerns come into conflict. One of those concerns here was constitutionally explicit, the prevention of double jeopardy. The opposing concern was so fundamental that it required no formal statement: public safety. A careful constitutional interpreter, faced with this 1937 controversy, is indeed directed to ponder the public conscience — but, at the same time, to afford a formal statement of that conscience by a local legislature a presumption of validity.

Here we may fairly accuse the Justices of 1937 of less than full and exacting attention to the Constitution. But if they read the letter carelessly, if they read it unhistorically, in their ruling they remained true to its spirit. They did not dictate to every state in the nation a debatable notion of fair procedure in criminal trials. They did not expect to extract from the Constitution an answer to every question, or a resolution of every conflict. They directed the gaze of conscience outward, toward their fellow citizens.

The Justices of 1937 did not, at least not expressly, direct the gaze of conscience upward toward Divinity, where Madison had directed it in his Memorial and Remonstrance. They spent no effort examining the motives of the local legislators who had given expression to the public conscience in Connecticut. And they refrained from lecturing or instructing those legislators.

Had the Court's gaze of conscience been lowered, in some sense, between the founding era and 1937?

The classification of different ways or styles of reasoning about conscience, about the rhetoric of conscientiousness if you will, is probably best left to philosophers and theologians. We can say here that the reasoning of these Supreme Court Justices in 1937, if it was not theological, was fundamentally republican in character. Their thought and their ruling accorded well with American political and constitutional tradition.

* * *

Several decades later, during the political unrest arising out of American military engagements in Southeast Asia, new opportunities arose for the Supreme Court to consider again the meaning and the legal significance of conscience. In 1965, for example, three young men who were fighting a summons to military service succeeded in getting their cases before the

Court. Each of them left the Court with an exemption from combat duty; and together, they elicited from the Justices some very interesting reasoning.[17]

Congress, as part of its governance of the armed forces, had long allowed such an exemption for some conscripts who refused to engage in armed conflict. Originally the privilege had been limited to members of a recognized religious sect whose doctrines included pacifism. Over the course of the twentieth century, however, the qualification had been relaxed somewhat. As of 1965, the statute made exemption available to persons whose religious training and belief had taught them conscientious objection to participation in war in any form. The requirement of church membership had been dropped. Congress, however, still denied exemption to those objecting on the basis of essentially political, sociological, or philosophical grounds; or, those pleading a merely personal moral code.

None of the young men before the Court in 1965 seemed to quite fit the statutory criteria. The Justices, however, ruling in their favor, came up with a somewhat different test for local draft authorities to use. If, they said, the objector's statement of conscience occupies "the same place in the life of the objector as an orthodox belief in God holds in the life of one clearly qualified for the exemption," then the exemption should be granted.

Note the peculiar position in which the Justices' new standard placed the officials of local draft boards. The officers reviewing a claimant's request for exemption were to weigh the conscience standing before them, so to speak; to put it in the scale against the conscience of a traditional theist. That seems quite a lot to expect of any public official. It seems suspiciously like a demand for clairvoyance or omniscience. What measure should a thoughtful hearing officer use? Mustn't he be quite reluctant to pronounce a judgment so difficult to make and defend?

Congressmen, presumably speaking for their constituents, had sought to ground legitimate conscientious objection in some broader social element, in some consensus of judgment on

---

[17] United States v. Seeger, 380 U.S. 163 (1965)

the part of more than a few persons. Congress had sought, that is, to avoid vesting in each individual, in effect, the discretion to participate in a war or not. It was not clear whether the Justices of 1965, in pointing toward a parallel to religion, or an analogy with theism, either respected or preserved that distinction. It was not clear in 1965 that the Justices stopped short of empow-ering each individual to strike his own balance between the sanctity of human life and his duty to defend his community.

The Justices, let us say, seemed to be turning the gaze of conscience inward; whereas Madison, in 1785, had turned that gaze upward, toward Divinity. The 1937 Court had turned that gaze outward, toward fellow citizens. But in 1965 introspection seemed to be gaining a firmer foothold in the American jurispru-dence of conscience.

This turn inward appeared again five years later, in another Supreme Court case involving a young man summoned to compulsory military service. His petition made quite plain the personal and philosophical character of his pacifism. In 1970 the Court nonetheless awarded him conscientious objector status.[18] The Justices found it sufficient that he held his views "with the strength of more traditional religious convictions." The Justices effectively abandoned any attempt to distinguish religious assertions of conscience from secular, or non-religious, asser-tions. They directed the gaze of conscience sharply inward, making any probing of alleged torment very awkward and diffi-cult, if not impractical.

* * *

Soon enough the implications of unrestrained judicial reasoning about conscience became a little clearer. In 1983 the Justices invoked the idea to support their correction of what they considered a moral misjudgment, or a moral abdication, on the part of Congress.[19]

The origin of this unusual judicial action was found in a provi-sion of the nation's tax code, one which had been the subject of litigation since 1970. Few taxpayer complaints, probably, reach

---

[18] Welsh v. United States, 398 U.S. 333 (1970)
[19] Bob Jones University v. United States, 461 U.S. 574 (1983)

down into the deepest moral strata. This case did. This was no ordinary wrangling over money.

The controversy had begun when the nation's tax collector, the Internal Revenue Service, changed its interpretation of a statute of long standing. Under the original enactment, educational institutions of all kinds had been routinely granted various exemptions which lightened their financial burdens and enabled them to raise funds more easily. On the basis of a new regulation, however, the IRS notified a few schools that they would no longer enjoy those privileges; and one of the schools responded with a suit seeking the restoration of its accustomed tax status.

The small college in question, a private one, had become something of an oddity in its time. As American public opinion was undergoing a fundamental change, the college's leaders had lagged behind. The Bible, as understood by the Christian sect which ran the school, was not entirely neutral as to the role of race in human affairs. Although students of all races were admitted, there were, on campus, certain limits imposed upon their social interaction. This contrariety, quite provocative when the nation was renewing its commitment to racial equality, could hardly pass unnoticed. The attentions of hostile politicians and civil rights organizations ensured that the dissenters would not be left in peace at the margins of a vast educational establishment.

It took thirteen years for the Supreme Court to validate the IRS's new regulation. That long-delayed conclusion may have been just, on balance. Yet the case posed troublesome questions, even if justice was served.

Why?

Because the religious character of the controversy was impossible to miss. The Government of the United States was engaged in penalizing the exercise of religious convictions. The Justices, all of them, were forthright about that. Both the majority and the lone dissenter agreed that Congress, in granting financial privileges to educational and other charitable organizations, has enough latitude in doing so to further vitally important public policies. Sufficient latitude, indeed, to discourage some religiously motivated conduct.

So far, so good. Racial equality, in education and more broadly, had certainly by this time become a clear and compelling national policy. The case report could have been ever so short and simple — if Congress had actually written anything about racial equality into the tax exemption statute at issue.

Congress, however, had not done so. Congressmen had discussed doing so, and some had introduced bills for that purpose. But Congress, despite ample time to act, had not changed the law.

Where, then, did the IRS get its authority to revise a long-settled legal interpretation?

The dissenter answered clearly. The IRS, he said, had no such authority; and the 1970 change, an initiative on the part of administrators only, should be struck down. If Congress wanted the college penalized, then Congress should speak. Until that occurred, he said, the college was entitled to equal tax treatment.

Eight Justices, however, disagreed with him. Eight Justices said that there was a proper legal foundation for what the IRS had done. Eight Justices said, or implied, that regardless of what Congress had done formally, or had not done formally, the nation's law needed to be brought into conformity with the nation's conscience.

Eight Justices declared, in effect, that the Court would act here as the interpreter, the ultimate if not the first interpreter, of the national conscience.

* * *

Probably most Americans, by the 1970s, would have agreed that racial equality in any educational setting is more than merely desirable. Many, perhaps, might have even have said that it is sacred. How many would have gone further, however, and agreed that a refusal to be racially color-blind, even in a private setting, is legally profane? How many would have said that such offenders should suffer a financial penalty in educating their children?

This new duty taken up by the Justices in 1983 would apparently have the Court drawing for the entire nation the demarcations between the sacred, the mundane, and the profane.

Sufficiently attentive Americans should not have been surprised at this. Only a decade earlier, the Court had declared itself, in so many words, the soul of the nation.[20] The Justices of 1973 had attempted an answer — a partial and negative answer, but important nonetheless — to a question to be found at the heart of every religion: "What is a human being?" At that time they had felt compelled to erect a façade of constitutional interpretation around their ruling; but few students of the Constitution had taken them seriously. Ten years later they felt no need for a facade. In one of those rare instances where Congress could properly make a religious judgment for the nation, where Congress actually needed to make a religious judgment for the nation — and where Congress was, in effect, doing so — the Justices openly usurped that authority and responsibility.

Note the irony here. By the late twentieth century the Justices had turned back, in a sense, to the view of James Madison. They were telling citizens of the United States, as had Madison, to look upward for guidance about sacred concerns. By upward, however, the Justices now meant toward the Court.

What remained, by this time, for the Court to accomplish?

---

[20] Roe v. Wade, 410 U.S. 113 (1973)

CHAPTER SIX: MYTHOPOESIS

The literatures of long ago offer us a wealth of colorful myths. There we read about the most remarkable changes in form, including the human form. Various persons, male and female, are there said to have become plants, or animals, or stars; even, in some cases, a god or goddess. These tales make pleasurable reading for those so inclined. Some scholars find them not only interesting, but also a source of insights into human nature and the human condition.

We err, however, if we think mythmaking has no allure today. There are practitioners among us at work. Literature is probably their most commonly and most consciously chosen setting. Some more daring souls, however, raise the banner of science over their work; and if we have doubts about their self-awareness, we should not begrudge them a word of praise for their creativity. Some can bend to their purposes the most unpromising ideas.

For example: We are now being told by an avant-garde among the new mythologists that men can become women, and women can become men.

This surely signifies, if nothing else, a stubbornly human resistance to convention and conformity. Here we see apparently thoughtful people, well along into an age of triumphant scientific materialism, proclaiming the transcendence of mind over matter, of psychology over biology. In a sense it is heartening to see such stalwart dissenters defying the world, even if we consider them fantasists. It is surely surprising, however, to find a prominent judicial tribunal endorsing, even implicitly or indirectly, their strange assertions. And it is more than merely surprising; it is disheartening to see respected jurists incorporating such notions into the public policy of a major modern nation.

The Supreme Court of the United States has done this.[21]

* * *

To this novel social phenomenon called "transgender," let us admit a certain narrow plausibility — if gender is taken to mean a fashion of style and dress, or a pattern of behavior, or a way of life. But the most zealous warriors against the male-female dichotomy scorn so modest an understanding. They insist that a transgender male truly is a female; and vice-versa. They force us to ask: Really?

Why should anyone accept so implausible a claim at face value?

We cannot tell from the Justices' opinion that this question of truth or falsehood troubled any of them, despite the majority's acknowledgment of the wide-spread surprise and dismay likely to be the result of their decision: "We can't deny that today's holding — that employers are prohibited from firing employees on the basis of homosexuality or transgender status — is an elephant."

Was the question of truth somehow beside the point? How could that be so?

The majority argued that they were simply deriving from civil rights legislation enacted in 1964 a compelling inference: that the Congressmen of that year, when the distinction between male and female was universally regarded as clear, fundamental, and immutable, nonetheless somehow committed the nation, by using the word sex, to the eventual obfuscation of that previously-unquestioned distinction.

---

[21] Bostock v. Clayton County, docket number 17-1618 (2020)

But simply to state the argument clearly is to see that it fails. And if men cannot actually become women, nor women men, then the Court's 2020 ruling depicts the Congress of 1964 as the sponsor of an elaborate and mandatory charade.

The Court, in other words, legislated, quite aggressively, once again. And this time they managed an additional feat of perversity. They put in place a law and a policy which neither Congress nor the Court had formally deliberated and endorsed. For the majority Justices insisted that they were doing nothing more than probing carefully the meaning of a phrase, sexual discrimination. They did not trouble themselves to argue that compliance with their mandate would advance the cause of justice. They seem to have assumed that if they fit their legal novelty into the customary framework of civil rights, it could not turn out to be a civil wrong.

Altogether this was a thoroughly embarrassing judicial episode.

* * *

Legislators ought always to be concerned with truth and falsehood. In general, surely, we want our laws and public policies to be grounded in truth. Official indifference to so important an inquiry is alarming.

There is a very old name for a myth considered too important and too salutary to be openly denied or mocked: a noble lie. Do we need noble lies today? Perhaps. But surely it is odd to find a supposedly constitutional court, staffed by professional lawyers, participating in the effort to provide them.

The originator of a myth may be innocent of any political motive. He or she may be simply exploring the riches of an exceptionally fertile imagination. There can be great satisfaction in the labor of articulating a fascinating tale. Then there may be attention, and honor, and even wealth for the spinner of a widely admired narrative. Subsequent authors who expand or elaborate may be similarly motivated.

What about those who disseminate a myth, carrying it to distant locations and new populations? Here, surely, purposes may become more varied and ambiguous. These actors may well be merchants of mythology, so to speak; their incentives are likely less artistic and more material. But they may also be serious moralists. They may be convinced that salutary lessons or deep insights are embedded in an appealing symbolic form. Successful mythopoesis can become an effective means of cultural and religious formation.

When this happens, some persons will inevitably be tempted to enhance their cultural authority, so to speak. Some will seek to endow a favored or useful myth with the power of convention and compulsion. Here motives shift toward the political side of the spectrum. Here indoctrination, mandatory celebrations, and official persecutions will follow. The pressure upon skeptics — there will always be skeptics — can become intense, even deadly.

Where along this spectrum shall we place the Supreme Court's contribution to the transgender cause? The Justices have given its central assertion the force of law and the status of a national orthodoxy. This is hardly a secondary or incidental contribution. What if the proselytizers of transgender are mistaken? What if their new faith only beguiles vulnerable people with false hopes? Neither living in falsehood nor persecuting stubborn truth-tellers seems a likely prescription for good health, either in individuals or the communities in which they live.

* * *

One of the Greek and Roman myths foreshadowed this development, perhaps. It told of a god and a goddess who merged into one so effectively that the new being could not be classified as male or female. But the two gods in question required the help of other gods in order to effect the transformation. In our up-to-date version, we ourselves can bring about the metamorphosis.

Apparently our entrance into what we like to call our secular and enlightened age has advanced somewhat less than we think. We see, if we know how to look, bitter contests for minds and souls taking place in a variety of settings. Even, wonder to behold, in the highest court of the American Republic.

Such struggles may be inevitable and perennial. Perhaps we need to acknowledge among the facets of human nature not only Homo sapiens but also — and of no lesser rank — Homo fabulator.

Postscript

Man the mythmaker, Homo fabulator, is surely no stranger to another familiar character, Homo religiosus. The hunger for meaning is deep-rooted. Mythology is one response, but there are others. Students of history may be struck by the way in which novel stories, images, ideas, or a creative gloss upon older ones, can set in motion a great deal more than words and symbols. New hopes can become widely enticing, latent tensions can be strengthened, long-suppressed resentments can flare up. Sometimes what seems in retrospect a kind of obsession or hysteria can erupt. Whole regions and populations can suddenly be plunged into prolonged turmoil, leaving later generations puzzled as to what seemed so plausible or so promising to so many.

An ancient example would be the rise and rapid expansion of Islam in the seventh century of the Common Era. Also, perhaps, somewhat less ancient, the counterattacks first launched by Christian Europe in the eleventh century.

Consider more recently the Protestant Reformation. It began in 1517 as a local rebellion against the powerful and wealthy Catholic Church, then spread across much of Europe, initiating some thirteen decades of widespread war and devastation.

In the 1790s came the French Revolution, which generated about two decades of military conflict and millions of deaths across Europe. It too was driven by religious zeal, or anti-religious zeal; for the Jacobins who were its avant-garde were intensely hostile to Christianity. But the Jacobins themselves were mythmakers. They were naïvely but fervently convinced that their new ways of thinking would bring about an age of universal liberty and fraternity and equality.

During the nineteenth century socialism took on a religious character. By dressing it up in pseudo-history and pseudo-science, its most famous prophet greatly strengthened its appeal to the credulous. After a few false starts the socialist true believers finally, early in the twentieth century, began to succeed; first convulsing, later controlling a large part of the globe. The cost in lives was tens of millions. Their major empires either collapsed or evolved into something quite different before the end of the same century, but scattered outposts and agitators still cling to the tattered dream.

* * *

Of making myths, as of the proverbial making books, there is no end. No doubt the discernment of patterns in history often bears a touch, perhaps more than a touch, of imagination. Risking fabulation nonetheless, I will suggest one such pattern.

The student of history mentioned above might reasonably conclude that outbreaks of ideological fury have accelerated their tempo over the last five centuries. He might venture a partial explanation. He might argue that whereas in antiquity, and in the Middle Ages, events were driven mainly by the forceful leadership of exceptional characters, ideology has now become the motor of change. The fifteenth-century invention of mechanized printing, enabling swift and wide distribution of the written word, provides a clue. Novel ideas, propagated by an articulate and charismatic visionary, can be very powerful, even intoxicating. This new capability played no small part in Martin Luther's success in bringing to a boil simmering resentments of the Catholic Church's corruptions and high-handed-ness. And thereafter the reach and rapidity of communications only continued to accelerate, surely playing no minor part in subsequent upheavals.

* * *

One of those subsequent upheavals was the American Revo-lution; but it was an upheaval with a difference. For the war it launched, that of thirteen British colonies in North America against their mother country, lasted only about five years; and it generated fewer deaths, by an order of magnitude, than the Protestant Reformation or the French and Bolshevik Revolu-tions. It was shorter and less lethal, and we might reasonably inquire why.

That the American war for independence wore the appear-ance of a merely political rebellion is no adequate answer. The statesmen who organized their countrymen and built a new nation also set loose among themselves and around the globe more than one new and counterintuitive idea. Their bold decla-ration of the essential equality of all human beings was rapidly disseminated. That principle, human equality, is more a reli-gious than a political proposition; for its irremediable ambi-guity opens to the faithful a bewildering variety of egalitarian paths to follow.

Nor was that all. Novel also, and no less counterintuitive to most, was the American assertion that religious liberty can be effectually universal; that religious dissensions and passions can be managed peacefully within the boundaries of one civic and political framework. That, in itself, is no less a religious conjecture.

The American founders managed an additional and remark-able feat: They wrote a Constitution that laid out a carefully considered, detailed, and pragmatic program for the attain-ment of both civic equality and religious liberty. The fate of that program of civic accommodation has been the subject of the preceding chapters.

The prognosis, unfortunately, cannot be considered favorable. The conceit of Supreme Court Justices that they can regulate religion in a neutral manner, a misunderstanding taking firm hold of the Court in the mid-twentieth century, has led to the Court's issuance of quite a number of new orthodoxies to be respected and observed throughout the United States. The character of these new orthodoxies has become increasingly problematic. Given expression in a misleading terminology of rights, they systematically diminish the most fundamental right of citizens in a republic — that of equal participation, as voters, in the formulation of public policy. Nor can the words used and the rationalizations offered conceal the highly contentious nature of the cultural and religious innovations being forced upon dissenting citizens.

Out of the calamitous sixteenth and seventeenth centuries in Europe came a formula for the restoration and maintenance of an uneasy peace: cuius regio, eius religio. The prince's religion is the people's religion. The American founders, while reversing that principle — the people's religion was to be the government's religion — preserved the geographical diversity which was implicit in both versions. But the Justices of the nation's Supreme Court, in the mid-twentieth century, began to apply the terms of the First Amendment against the local governments. They upended a century and a half of their jurisprudence of religion by enlarging the application of the first sixteen words of the First Amendment beyond the strict terms of the constitutional text.[22]

The Justices, unwittingly, thereby reconstituted themselves as a religious aristocracy. They began to act as spiritual princes to the American nation. They boldly proclaimed as their goal a political order purged of religious judgments. But that is an impossible dream. As well try to remove a foundation while leaving the building sited upon it in place. The Court has yet to reflect publicly and thoughtfully upon that fateful change of constitutional course.

---

[22] See Hamilton v. Regents of the University of California, 293 U.S. 245 (1934)

The time for reflection is more than overdue. Religious resentments and conflicts now roil the Republic ceaselessly — and make their way to the Court. The Reformation strikes us as a historical curiosity, if we think of it at all; even as we watch a new Reformation unfold around us. Indeed, struggles over human nature, human flourishing, and human destiny have been globalized, along with economies and cultures. And never have the competing visions been more heterogeneous.

The ambition of bringing whole populations into some favored spiritual and moral and behavioral conformity is ancient and perhaps inextinguishable. If not always futile, it seems to have become so. The history lesson has been forgotten, but it needs to be relearned; sooner, we must hope, rather than later. Those venerable statesmen of Philadelphia, two and a quarter centuries ago, pointed out a promising way for quite different communities to live together amicably. Their political posterity, however, have been failing to heed them for decades.

Printed in the United States
by Baker & Taylor Publisher Services